Biomes Atlases

TROPICAL GRASSLANDS

Ben Morgan

Raintree

Raintree

www.raintreepublishers.co.uk

Phone 44 (0) 1865 888112
Send a fax to 44 (0) 1865 314091
Visit the Raintree bookshop online at www.raintreepublishers.co.uk
to browse our catalogue and order online.

First published in Great Britain in 2003 by Raintree, Halley Court,
Jordan Hill, Oxford, OX2 8EJ, part of Harcourt Education Ltd.
Raintree is a registered trademark of Harcourt Education Ltd.
Copyright © 2003 The Brown Reference Group plc.

Printed and bound in Singapore.

ISBN 1 844 21159 2
07 06 05 04 03
10 9 8 7 6 5 4 3 2 1

British Library Cataloging-in-Publication Data

A full catalogue is available for this book from the British Library.

The Brown Reference Group plc
Project Editor: Ben Morgan
Deputy Editor: Dr. Rob Houston
Copy-editors: John Farndon and Angela Koo
Consultant: Dr. Mark Hostetler, Department
    of Wildlife Ecology and Conservation,
    University of Florida
Designer: Reg Cox
Cartographers: Mark Walker and
    Darren Awuah
Picture Researcher: Clare Newman
Indexer: Kay Ollerenshaw
Managing Editor: Bridget Giles
Design Manager: Lynne Ross
Production: Alastair Gourlay

Raintree Publishers
Editors: Isabel Thomas and Kate Buckingham

Front cover: Acacia tree on the East
African savanna.
Inset: Cheetah chasing a young gazelle.

Title page: Elephants and Mount Kilimanjaro
in Amboseli National Park, Kenya.

The acknowledgments on p. 64 form
part of this copyright page. Every effort has
been made to contact copyright holders of
any material reproduced in this book. Any
omissions will be rectified in subsequent
printings if notice is given to the publishers.

About this book

The introductory pages of this book describe the world's biomes and then the tropical grassland biome. The five main chapters look at aspects of tropical grasslands: climate, plants, animals, people and future. Between the chapters are detailed maps that focus on key grassland regions. The map pages are shown in the contents in italics, **like this**.

Throughout the book you'll also find boxed stories or fact files about tropical grasslands. The icons here show what the boxes are about. At the end of the book is a glossary, which explains what all the difficult words mean. After the glossary is a list of books and websites for further research and an index, allowing you to locate subjects anywhere in the book.

 Climate

 People

 Plants

 Future

 Animals

 Facts

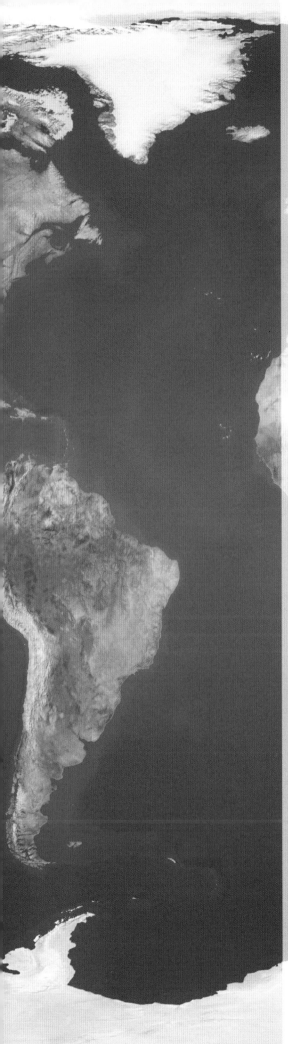

00518465

Contents

Biomes of the world

Biologists divide the living world into major zones called biomes. Each biome has its own distinctive climate, plants and animals.

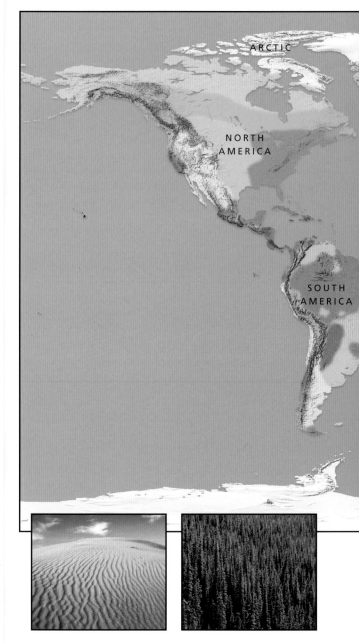

I f you were to walk all the way from the north of Canada to the Amazon **rainforest**, you'd notice the wilderness changing dramatically along the way.

Northern Canada is a freezing and barren place without trees, where only tiny brownish-green plants can survive in the icy ground. But trudge south for long enough and you enter a magical world of conifer forests, where moose, caribou (reindeer) and wolves live. After several weeks, the conifers disappear, and you reach the grass-covered prairies of the central USA. The further south you go, the drier the land gets and the hotter the sun feels, until you find yourself hiking through a cactus-filled **desert**. But once you reach southern Mexico, the cacti start to disappear, and strange **tropical** trees begin to take their place. Here, the muggy air is filled with the calls of exotic birds and the drone of tropical insects. Finally, in Colombia you cross the Andes mountain range – whose chilly peaks remind you a little of your starting point – and descend into the dense, swampy jungles of the Amazon rainforest.

Desert is the driest biome. There are hot deserts and cold ones.

Taiga is made up of conifer trees that can survive freezing winters.

Scientists have a special name for the different regions – such as desert, tropical rainforest and prairie – that you'd pass through on such a journey. They call them **biomes**. Everywhere on Earth can be classified as being in one biome or another, and the same biome often appears in lots of

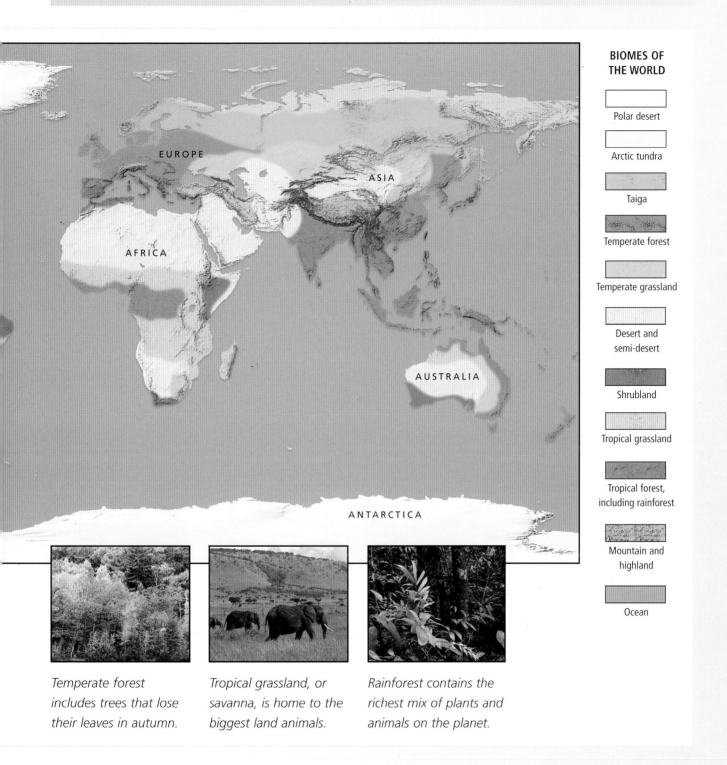

BIOMES OF
THE WORLD

Polar desert

Arctic tundra

Taiga

Temperate forest

Temperate grassland

Desert and
semi-desert

Shrubland

Tropical grassland

Tropical forest,
including rainforest

Mountain and
highland

Ocean

EUROPE

ASIA

AFRICA

AUSTRALIA

ANTARCTICA

*Temperate forest
includes trees that lose
their leaves in autumn.*

*Tropical grassland, or
savanna, is home to the
biggest land animals.*

*Rainforest contains the
richest mix of plants and
animals on the planet.*

different places. For instance, there are areas of rainforest as far apart as Brazil, Africa and South-east Asia. Although the plants and animals that inhabit these forests are different, they live in similar ways. Likewise, the prairies of North America are part of the grassland biome, which also occurs in China, Australia and Argentina. Wherever there are grasslands, there are grazing animals that feed on the grass, as well as large **carnivores** that hunt and kill the **grazers**.

The map on this page shows how the world's major biomes fit together to make up the biosphere – the zone of life on Earth.

5

Earth's tropical grasslands

About 40 per cent of the land in Earth's tropical zone is covered by grass or a mix of grass and other plants. Such areas form the tropical grassland biome.

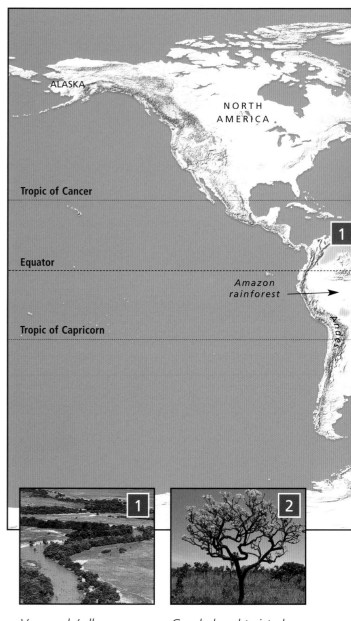

Venezuela's llanos grasslands are riddled with forest-lined rivers.

Gnarled and twisted trees typify Brazil's hot Cerrado savanna.

Earth's tropical zone is the area between the **tropics of Cancer** and **Capricorn** – two imaginary circles drawn around the planet 2600 km (1600 miles) north and south of the **equator**. In parts of the tropics that are too dry for forest but too wet for desert or **shrubland**, grasslands thrive.

Tropical grasslands often have a scattering of trees, forming a landscape called **savanna**. Most areas of tropical grassland are like this, so the terms savanna and tropical grassland are often used interchangeably. Where the trees get close enough to form a closed **canopy**, the grass disappears and the savanna merges into the **tropical forest** biome.

The biggest area of tropical grassland is in Africa, where flat-topped trees called **acacias** dot the plains. Africa's savannas are home to gigantic plant-eaters such as elephants and giraffes, vast herds of grass-eating antelope and some of the world's most dangerous carnivores, including lions and hyenas.

South America has two large areas of tropical grassland: the llanos and the Cerrado. Both are mainly savanna, but instead of acacias there are palms or short, gnarled trees. Surprisingly, there are few large animals that live only in the grasslands of South America – most also live in the neighbouring tropical forests or shrublands.

In the dry Sahel of Africa, herding cattle is an important way of life.

Hyenas and other large carnivores prowl the savannas of East Africa.

Some people still live off wild foods in northern Australia's grasslands.

In the savannas of northern Australia, **eucalyptus** trees take the place of acacias, and kangaroos replace antelope. Australia's savanna forms a transition zone between the forests of the north and the central desert. As you travel south across it, the forest thins out and gives way to grassland, which in turn peters out into desert.

The map above shows the biggest areas of tropical grassland, but there are also small patches of tropical grassland mixed in with other biomes. There are even patches of savanna in the heart of the Amazon rainforest. Some people also consider most of India to be a kind of artificial savanna, formed long ago by **deforestation**.

Llanos

Stretching across northern South America is a huge lowland plain filled with a mixture of wetlands and grasslands – the llanos.

The skills of the llanos's cowboys, or llaneros, are useful when hunting capybaras, the giant rodents of the area. Capybara meat is salted, dried and eaten during Easter.

Giant anteater

The llanos are home to more than their fair share of giants, including giant snakes (anacondas) and giant rodents (capybaras). But perhaps the most spectacular is the giant anteater, which looks all the larger for its enormous bushy tail and disproportionately long snout. Giant anteaters are fussy eaters, feeding exclusively on ants and termites. After using their sharp front claws to dig a hole into an ant or termite nest, they poke their long, toothless snout inside and gather prey with a sticky tongue.

The tongue can extend up to 60 cm (24 in) and flicks in and out up to three times a second, gathering grubs and pupae as well as adults. Giant anteaters walk on their knuckles, keeping their front claws curved inwards so they don't dig into the ground. They are solitary animals, though youngsters ride on their mothers' backs for up to a year after birth.

Caribbean Sea

NETHERLANDS ANTILLES

GRENADA

Atlantic Ocean

Caribbean Sea

Port of Spain
TRINIDAD AND TOBAGO

Barranquilla

Golfo de Venezuela

2

Caracas

SOUTH AMERICA

PANAMA

Cristóbal Colón Peak

Maracaibo Lake

VENEZUELA

6 Orinoco Delta

Cordillera de Mérida

Bolívar Peak

1

Apure River

Aguaro-Guariquito National Park

4

Llanos de Apure

3

Orinoco River

5

Georgetown

Cinaruco-Capanaparo National Park

Embalse de Guri

7

Caroní River

GUYANA

Pacaraima Mountains

Essequibo River

N

Bogotá

El Tuparro National Park

Guiana Highlands

Roraima

Angel Falls

9

10

Cali

Meta River

COLOMBIA

8

Rupununi savanna

La Macarena National Park

Pico da Neblina

BRAZIL

Equator

11

Amazon Basin

Negro River

Manaus

1. Andes mountains
This chain of mountains on the west of South America marks the western limit of the llanos.

2. Caribbean coast
Grassland gives way to hilly shrubland and tropical dry forest along the northern coast of Venezuela. Moist forest flourishes on the mountains.

3. Llanos de Apure
An almost tree-less flooded savanna in the centre of the llanos, home to roseate spoonbills, anacondas and many other wetland animals.

4. Aguaro-Guariquito National Park
A 0.6-million-hectare (about 1.5-million-acre) protected area of savanna and wetland, inhabited by pumas, jaguars, giant anteaters and capybaras.

5. Orinoco River
The main river draining the llanos. Its western tributaries include the Guaviare, Meta and Apure Rivers.

6. Orinoco Delta
A complex mosaic of swamp forest, mangroves and grassland. In the dry season, agoutis and pacas comb the forest floor for seeds; in the wet season, crocodiles and otters take their place when the delta floods.

7. Embalse de Guri
A gigantic reservoir formed in 1986 by construction of a hydroelectric plant on the Caroní River.

8. Guiana Highlands
A wild area of highlands, formed from very ancient crystalline rock and covered with savanna and rainforest. Famous for flat-topped mountains called tepuis.

9. Angel Falls
The world's highest waterfall, at 979 metres (3212 ft) tall. The water plunges down the side of a tepui called Devil's Mountain, barely making contact with the sheer face as it falls.

10. Rupununi savanna
Distinct from the llanos, this remote area of tropical grassland is surrounded by rainforest. The dominant plant here is grass because the sandy soil and high ground cannot hold enough water for trees.

11. Amazon Basin
The world's largest river basin, mostly filled with dense tropical rainforest.

Fact file

▲ The llanos lie between the Andes mountains, the Caribbean Sea and the Guiana Highlands. Their total area is about 570,000 square km (220,000 sq miles) – bigger than all of France.

▲ The land is mostly savanna, but dense forest borders the rivers. Treeless areas of swamp grasses and sedges are common in low-lying areas.

▲ The llanos receive more rain than most tropical grasslands. Rainfall varies from 1000 mm (39 in) in the east to 4570 mm (180 in) near the Andes. The dry season lasts 5–6 months in the east but only 1–2 months in the south-west.

▲ The Amazon Basin contains islands of savanna, called campos, where the soil is too sandy, stony or marshy for trees to grow.

Pacific Ocean

Andes

BOLIVIA

0   200   miles
0   200   400 km

Grassland climate

Tropical grasslands mostly occur in warm countries with marked wet and dry seasons. However, there are many factors besides climate that influence where tropical grasslands grow.

Right: The sun sets over the savanna of East Africa. Day turns to night surprisingly quickly near the equator, the sun sinking straight down at about 6 p.m. every day.

After the dinosaurs

Tropical grassland is one of the youngest biomes. During the age of the dinosaurs, there was no such thing as grassland because grass plants hadn't evolved. Plant-eating dinosaurs probably ate ferns, conifer trees and palm-like plants called cycads.

Scientists know from fossil evidence that grass plants had appeared by about 50 million years ago, but it was another 30 million or so years before savannas formed, starting in South America. In the last 20 million years, Earth's climate has become cooler and drier. As a result, the lush forests that once covered the tropics have shrunk, and tropical grasslands have expanded in their place.

In the rainforest of central Africa, the weather is hot and humid all year round. Winter doesn't exist, and the sun rises and sets at about the same time every day of the year. Travel north to the Sahara Desert, though, and things are different. Instead of cloudy skies and frequent downpours, the sky is a flawless blue, and it almost never rains. In summer it is unbearably hot – even in the middle of the night – but in winter the nights can be bitterly cold.

The African rainforest and the Sahara Desert both have their own distinctive pattern of weather through the year, which we call their **climate**. The rainforest has a constantly wet climate, the desert a constantly dry one. The climate of tropical grasslands is typically a mixture of the two: soaking wet for half the year and bone-dry for the rest.

The tropical zone

Climates are caused by the uneven way that sunlight warms our planet as we hurtle through space. The Earth spins like a top as it orbits the Sun, staying roughly upright. The equator faces the Sun directly, so it basks in strong sunshine every day of the year. The poles, on the other hand, get very little warmth. What sunlight they receive is spread over a wide area because of the Earth's curved shape, making the Sun's rays feeble. It's a bit like shining a torch on a wall: if you hold the torch at an angle, the beam spreads out and casts a weaker light.

Tropical grasslands are in the warm region near the equator, where the Sun's rays are most intense. They are part of the Earth's tropical zone – the region between the tropics of Capricorn and Cancer, two imaginary circles on either side of the equator. Outside the tropics is the Earth's **temperate** zone, where the weather is cooler.

Land in the tropics receives about five times more heat and energy per square mile than in the far north and south, so it isn't surprising the climate is much warmer. The average daytime temperature in tropical grasslands is usually more than 24°C (75°F), and it doesn't vary a great deal through the year. The steady, warm temperature gives plants and animals a great advantage over the wildlife of temperate grasslands, since they never have to deal with freezing winter weather. And the endless, intense sunshine makes plants grow quickly.

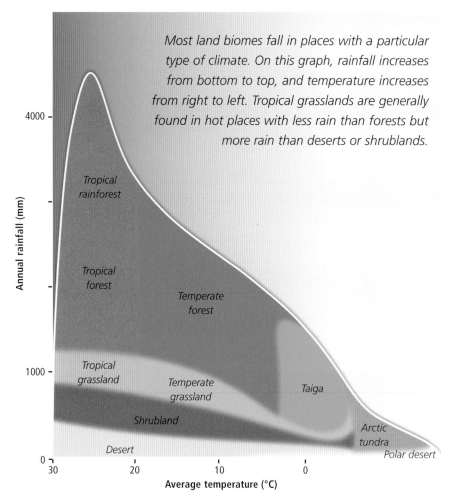

Most land biomes fall in places with a particular type of climate. On this graph, rainfall increases from bottom to top, and temperature increases from right to left. Tropical grasslands are generally found in hot places with less rain than forests but more rain than deserts or shrublands.

Annual rainfall (mm)

4000

Tropical rainforest

Tropical forest

Temperate forest

1000

Tropical grassland

Temperate grassland

Taiga

Shrubland

Arctic tundra

Desert

Polar desert

0

30   20   10   0

Average temperature (°C)

Rain belt

The Sun's energy doesn't just create warm weather in the tropics – it also produces rain. Sunlight warms the surface of the tropical oceans, filling the air with water vapour and making the weather humid and clammy. Because the air is warm, it rises into the sky, carrying the water vapour with it. As the water vapour rises, it cools, which makes it turn back into liquid and fall as rain. As a result, the Earth's equator is surrounded by a belt of warm and rainy weather – the climate that creates tropical rainforests.

The warm air that rises over the equator can't continue rising forever. When it cools high in the **atmosphere**, it stops rising and gets pushed

Grassland microclimates

Maps of the world's biomes give the impression that each biome covers a vast area without change, but the truth isn't so simple. Savanna is really a mosaic of forest and grassland, with the number of trees varying from place to place. Trees are most common in rainiest parts of the savanna, and sparse in drier areas. There are even patches of tropical forest right in the middle of the savanna. These grow in areas with an unusual microclimate – weather or conditions different from the surroundings. For instance,

wet riversides in the llanos of Venezuela (left) are often covered with trees, forming a habitat termed gallery forest. These strips of forest occur in most tropical grasslands and often contain the same types of trees that grow in tropical rainforests. Likewise, mountain tops are sometimes covered with cloud forests, which thrive on the fog that forms in cold, high air. In East Africa, an enormous volcanic crater called Ngorongoro has cloud forest around the rim but grassland in the centre.

away from the equator by the air rising behind it. Now cold and dry, the air begins to fall back down, sinking thousands of miles north and south of the equator. Because it no longer carries water vapour, it causes dry weather where it sinks. The world's major hot deserts, such as the Sahara in northern Africa, exist because of this sinking dry air.

Wet and dry seasons

If the Earth stayed completely upright as it orbited the Sun, the belts of equatorial rain and sinking dry air would always be in the same place. But the Earth is tipped over slightly, making it spin at an angle, and this is why there are seasons. During summer in the northern **hemisphere**, the North Pole tilts towards the Sun, causing warm, sunny weather and long days. In winter, it tilts away from the Sun, resulting in cold weather and long nights.

Earth's tilt also affects the climate in the tropics, but it produces wet and dry seasons instead of warm and cold ones. When the North Pole tilts towards the Sun, northern parts of the tropics become warmer than southern parts, so the belt of warm, rising air around the equator shifts north slightly, taking the rainy weather with it. For northern parts of the tropics, therefore, July is usually the middle of the rainy season. At the same time, southern parts of the tropics move into the zone of sinking, dry air, resulting in a dry season. In January the opposite happens: southern parts of the tropics are deluged with rain, while northern areas have a dry season.

Areas close to the equator stay under the belt of rainy weather nearly all year round, creating ideal conditions for tropical forests,

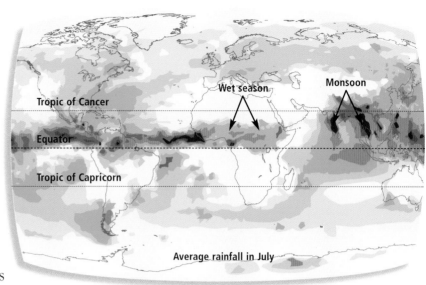

A belt of rainy weather (blue) surrounds the equator. It moves north in summer (above) and south in winter (below), creating wet and dry seasons.

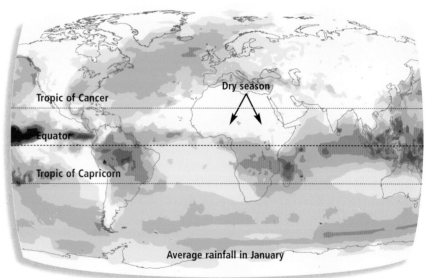

but the zones to the north and south of the forests have marked wet and dry seasons. As a result, grasslands are most common in the northern or southern parts of the tropics.

On average, tropical grasslands receive 1000–1500 mm (40–60 in) of rain a year. By comparison, deserts receive less than 250 mm (10 in), and rainforests may receive more than 2500 mm (100 in). However, there are also tropical grasslands in areas with much less or much more rain than the

13

average. A more important factor than total rainfall is the length of the dry season, which usually lasts five to seven months. If the dry season is any longer, the land is more likely to be shrubland or semi-desert; any shorter and forest takes over.

The severity of the dry season also matters. Tropical grasslands usually occur where the dry season brings weather as harsh as a desert's. Although some rain may fall, it quickly **evaporates** in the heat, leaving the ground parched and dusty. This harsh weather is stressful for plants, especially trees. In grasslands with a less severe dry season, trees can survive by shedding their leaves or becoming **dormant** (inactive). But in the driest tropical grasslands, only grasses survive.

Parts of Venezuela's llanos grasslands are flooded in the wet season. The temporary marshes provide perfect cover for giant anacondas – the world's biggest snakes.

Monsoons

Some parts of the world have an especially severe wet season called a monsoon. One of the most extreme monsoons occurs in India, which is drenched with rain every year from June to September.

The cause of a monsoon's intensity is the uneven warming of land and sea. Land warms up more quickly under strong sunlight than does the sea, making air rise faster above it. During the northern summer, the vast landmass of Asia heats up. The air over land absorbs this heat and rises, sucking in more air from the Indian Ocean like a giant vacuum cleaner. The air travelling from the ocean (called the monsoon wind) picks up moisture from the sea and dumps it on India as rain.

India's monsoon is so powerful that it draws moisture-bearing wind away from East Africa, creating a dry season in the savannas of East Africa – even though these grasslands lie on the equator, where tropical rainforests would normally prevail.

Even within one area of tropical grassland, the length of the dry season varies from place to place. The wettest places, in which trees are most common, are where the grassland borders tropical forest. As you travel across the grassland toward the desert biome, the dry season gets longer and the trees become sparse. In dry parts of the grassland, the rainy season is not only shorter but also less reliable. In some years, it fails to rain at all.

Breaking the rules

Although tropical grasslands generally occur in places with a marked dry season, they often break this rule. There are many patches of tropical grassland mixed in with other biomes, especially tropical forest. There are even patches of tropical grassland in the heart of the Amazon rainforest, where it rains nearly all year round.

The explanation for these rule-breaking patches of biome is that other factors besides climate determine where grasslands grow. One such factor, for instance, is soil

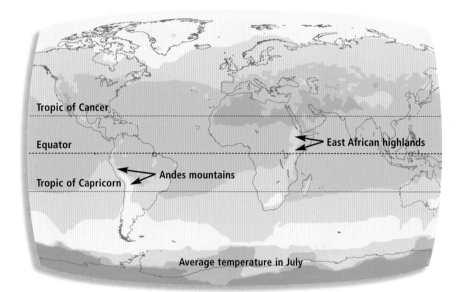

Most parts of the tropics stay warm all year round, shown by warm colours on these maps. Mountains are slightly cooler than lowlands.

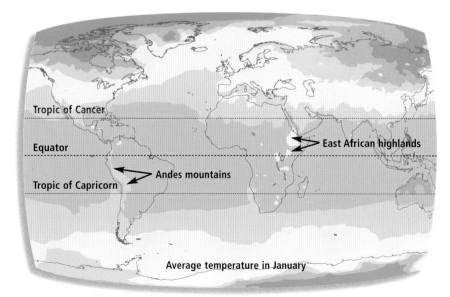

Unreliable rains

In many parts of the world, people take the seasons for granted. In North America, for instance, winter never fails to arrive, bringing cold weather and long nights. But in the tropics, the seasons are less reliable. The people and animals of tropical grasslands depend on the annual rainy season to bring back the rich grass, but sometimes the rains do not arrive. The result is a drought: the land turns to desert, animals die, crops wither and people may starve.

Some people blame droughts on global warming, but they are a natural part of the tropical grassland climate. The risk of drought has had an interesting effect on how the wildlife has evolved. Unlike the animals and plants of tropical forests, those of tropical grasslands tend to have short lives, but they mature quickly and produce more offspring. This means they can quickly recolonize the land after a severe drought has killed off most of the wildlife.

Climographs

Each place in the world has its own pattern of weather, or climate. We can sum up a place's climate on a climograph, such as the one shown here for St Louis in the USA (right). The letters along the bottom are the months of the year. The numbers on the left and the small bars show rainfall, and the numbers on the right and the curvy line show temperature. Unlike St Louis, most tropical grasslands (below) are hot all year round and have pronounced wet and dry seasons. Nairobi in Kenya has two wet seasons each year.

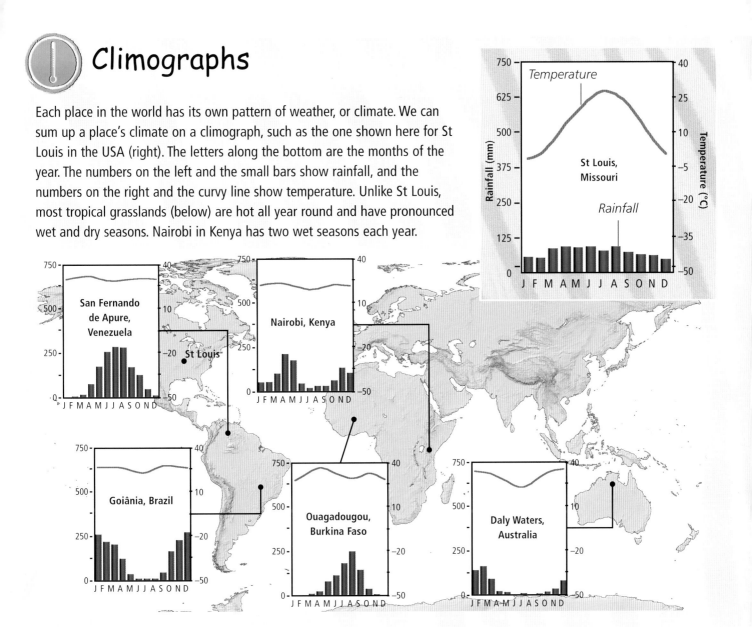

type. If the soil is too stony for trees, or if water drains through it too easily, grasses will flourish where there would otherwise be forest. The well-drained volcanic soil of the Serengeti in Africa is virtually tree-less in places for this reason. Likewise, grass takes over in areas that are so boggy that the soil becomes acidic and low in **nutrients** – many of the patches of grassland in the Amazon rainforest formed this way.

The soil in tropical countries is often red because of an insoluble chemical called iron oxide (rust), which tends to build up over time as the rain washes other chemicals away. Soils that are very rich in iron oxide are called laterites. They tend to bake solid under the tropical sun, forming a hardpan below the surface that blocks roots and so stops trees from growing. In the wet season, the hardpan traps water, making the ground too waterlogged for trees. Though some types of palm trees can survive in laterites, the plants that usually dominate are grasses.

Grassland fires

Another important factor is fire. Dry grass makes perfect kindling for wildfires in the dry season. Unless animals have nibbled the grass down to the ground, the continuous cover of grass spreads the fire over vast areas. The fire kills tree seedlings, but grass plants survive thanks to underground roots and shoots.

Mist often hangs over Africa's savannas in the cool early mornings. Lions and other big predators do most of their hunting during the night and around dawn, avoiding the stifling heat of the day.

Regular fires, therefore, can create grassland where there would otherwise be forest.

Fires start naturally during thunderstorms, which are common towards the end of the dry season. All it takes is a single dry lightning strike to set the land on fire. However, most tropical grassland fires are probably started by people, often deliberately. In the Sahel region of Africa, for instance, people have been burning grassland for more than 2500 years in order to clear trees and shrubs and thus create better grazing land for livestock. Today, an estimated 75 per cent of Africa's tropical grassland is burnt each year.

Animals, too, can turn forest into grassland. When grazing animals nibble tree seedlings, they kill the plants by biting off the buds. Grass plants, in contrast, have buds

Below: These termite mounds in northern Australia are called compass mounds because they always face east and west. This probably helps control the microclimate inside the mounds. During cool early mornings and late evenings, the mounds catch the warmth of the rising and setting sun, but at midday their thin shape catches much less sunlight, helping to prevent overheating.

Thunderstorms are common in the tropics, especially at the end of the dry season. If lightning strikes dry grass, it can trigger a wildfire.

nibble the grass very close to the ground, fires cannot spread; without fires to kill off bigger plants, trees and shrubs begin to take over.

Livestock and people have had such a big influence on tropical grasslands, and for so long, that it is often difficult to say which grasslands are natural or artificial. The truth is that most tropical grasslands are probably semi-natural, which means that human activity has been an important part of the biome's ecology for many thousands of years.

at the base of the plant or underground, so they quickly recover from grazing. However, excessive grazing can have the opposite effect, turning grassland into forest. If animals

 # Ancient fires

The Aboriginal people of Australia have probably been setting fire to the savanna since their ancestors arrived on the continent at least 50,000 years ago. While people in other parts of the world use fire to clear land for crops, Aborigines didn't begin farming until very recently. Instead, they used fire to flush animals out of the bush, or to clear scrub to make hunting and travelling easier. Before the arrival of Aborigines, the savanna region of Australia might have been covered with tropical forest. There are still patches of tropical forest in parts of the savanna that fire doesn't reach, such as volcanic crater floors and rocky gullies.

Cerrado

South and east of the Amazon Basin, the climate is too dry for rainforest. In its place is the Cerrado: the largest expanse of tropical grassland in the Americas.

Cerrado trees (right) look contorted because new growth starts each wet season from side buds.

 ## Fact file

▲ The Cerrado is a mosaic of savanna, shrubland and dry forest. Dense gallery forests border rivers.

▲ Thick, gnarled bark gives the Cerrado's trees protection against fire. In some tree species, up to two-thirds of the trunk's width is bark.

▲ There are at least 10,400 plant species, 180 reptile species, 837 bird species and 195 mammal species in the Cerrado. Many live nowhere else.

 ## Wolf on stilts

The maned wolf is the largest member of the dog family native to South America. Although called a wolf, it lives alone rather than in a pack, and it looks more like an elegant fox than a wolf. Its long legs help it peer over tall grass or bushes while hunting. Its prey, which it stalks and then leaps on with a stiff-legged pounce, include armadillos, pacas, rabbits and birds. However, more than half the maned wolf's diet consists of seasonal fruits, plant roots and bulbs. In Brazil, some people believe the animal has magical powers, including the ability to kill a chicken with its gaze. The left eye of a live wolf is sometimes cut out and kept as a good luck charm.

1. Gran Chaco
A dry shrubland area between the Cerrado and the Andes mountains, home to jaguars, pumas, tapirs, giant armadillos and numerous reptiles.

2. Chapada dos Guimarães National Park
This protected area lies in the transition zone between the Cerrado and the Amazon forest. Colourful toucans and macaws live among the park's cliffs, waterfalls and gallery forests.

3. Pantanal
A marshy depression grazed by cattle in the dry season but flooded in the wet season, leaving only hilltops exposed. Renowned for its beauty, the Pantanal is one of the world's largest freshwater wetlands and is a haven for wildlife.

4. Paraná River
South America's second longest river after the Amazon flows 4880 km (3032 miles) from the Brazilian Highlands to its mouth in the South Atlantic.

5. Itaipu dam
One of the largest hydroelectric plants in the world, jointly owned by Paraguay and Brazil. Its construction created a gigantic reservoir, completely submerging the once spectacular Guaíra Falls.

6. Iguaçú Falls
A dramatic, horseshoe-shaped waterfall where the Iguaçú River plunges off the Paraná Plateau into a deep gorge. National parks in both Brazil and Argentina protect the rich wildlife around the falls.

7. Emas National Park
A protected area of Cerrado with a mixture of shrubland, savanna and open grassland, dotted with brick-red termite mounds as tall as a person.

8. Brasília
The federal capital of Brazil, established in the 1950s. In the last 50 years, building and the spread of farming around both Brasília and the new highways serving the city have destroyed large areas of the Cerrado.

9. Brazilian Highlands
An area of rolling hills, deep valleys and plateaus, with an average height above sea level of 1000 metres (3300 ft).

10. Caatinga shrubland
Almost impenetrable thorny shrubland in the north-east, where the climate is very dry.

Grassland plants

Grassland plants are among the toughest plants on Earth. They can spring back to life after being starved of rain for months, chewed to stumps by animals and burnt to a crisp.

If you were to visit Africa's Serengeti grasslands twice in one year, you might get a surprise. In May, towards the end of the main rainy season, lush green grass carpets the ground as far as you can see. But in September, in the dry season, things could hardly be more different. What little grass remains has turned to straw, and the dusty ground looks like a desert.

The same thing happens in tropical grasslands in many other places. Every year, a blistering dry season drains the land of colour, and the grass shrivels under the relentless tropical sun. Yet when the rains return, the same desiccated plants somehow spring back to life and turn the landscape green again.

The plants of tropical grasslands spend around half the year living through desert conditions, but that's not the only challenge they face. In the dry season, they have to contend with raging wildfires, fuelled by the tinder-dry straw. And in the wet season, herds of grazing animals trample across them and eat them. To most plants, such constant hardship would be lethal. However, grass plants not only survive being maimed, burned and starved – they thrive on it.

A world of grass

The grass family is the success story of the plant world. Since grass plants first evolved a mere 50 million years ago, grasses have spread across the world and taken over vast swathes of land. One reason for their success was a gradual cooling and drying of the Earth's climate, which favoured drought-tolerant plants. Another reason was the recent appearance of a **species** that has a very special relationship with grasses: humans.

Grasses are expert colonizers, able to establish themselves quickly on disturbed land. As humans spread around the world, felling forests and changing the landscape,

 ## Photosynthesis

Like animals, plants cannot survive without food. Unlike animals, however, they don't have to eat – they can make food. Plants need only a few simple ingredients to make food: water, air and sunlight. Inside the cells that make up a plant's leaf (right) are tiny food-making factories called chloroplasts. These contain the green substance chlorophyll, which gives plants their colour. Chlorophyll captures energy from sunlight and uses it to combine water and carbon dioxide from air into food molecules.

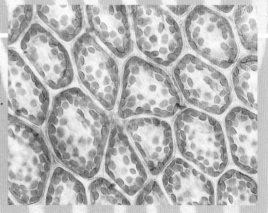

 # Bloated baobabs

The baobab trees of Africa, Madagascar and northern Australia are expert water storers. During the wet season, they soak up massive amounts of water and store it within soft, spongy wood inside the trunk and lower branches, which swell up like balloons. When the dry season begins, baobabs shed their leaves (which reduces water loss) and slowly draw on their hidden reserves; as the water gets used up, the trunk appears to shrink. Baobabs can cope with very long dry seasons and grow in semi-deserts as well as savanna. They grow slowly but reach enormous sizes. One hollow tree in Zimbabwe is large enough for up to forty people to shelter inside its trunk. Other baobabs have been used as a shop, a prison, a house and a bus shelter.

Tall grass makes a good hiding place for small animals, such as this klipspringer, a type of antelope from Africa.

Topsy-turvy plants

Have you ever mowed a lawn and wondered why the grass plants don't die when you cut them? In most plants, the growing parts (called meristems) are at the top, or inside buds next to branches. If you cut the stalk, you remove all the growing parts and the plant dies. Grasses are different: their growing parts are at the bottom instead of the top. When you mow a lawn, all you do is cut through the blades of grass, leaving behind the growing parts. New blades soon spring up.

The unusual position of the meristems helps grass survive constant munching by animals. In fact, grazing animals can help grass plants. Although they damage the grass blades, the grazers do more damage to other plants growing nearby. In the process,

Despite lacking front teeth, white rhinos nibble grass right to the ground with their lips. Yet grasses can survive even this drastic pruning.

grasses followed them. Grasses are the botanical equivalent of rats – wherever people live, you're sure to find grasses thriving in patches of wasteland and in nooks and crannies among buildings. But grasses are not just weeds – for thousands of years, humans have deliberately bred and grown grasses for their edible seeds. Cereal crops such as wheat, rice and corn, which together form the staple foods for most of the world's people, are the descendants of wild grasses. The seed heads of these plants have become grotesquely enlarged by years of careful breeding, so much so that they hardly look like grasses anymore.

The properties that make grasses successful weeds also equip them for life in tropical grasslands. The harsh dry season, regular fires and hordes of grass-eating animals continually disturb the land, just as human settlements disturb natural habitats. Grasses have evolved all sorts of features that overcome the constant trauma.

Jeepers creepers

Africa's tropical grasses are aggressive plants – so much so that they are taking over other parts of the world. Scientists have found that some parts of tropical America, where forests had been removed for agriculture, are now covered with such African grasses as paragrass, pangola grass and jaragua. In southern parts of the USA, one of the most common grasses in lawns and golf courses is Bermuda grass (right), an African savanna species that spreads by growing creepers (horizontal stems). Oddly enough, American grasses introduced into Africa have not had anything like the same success.

they clear the ground of competition, allowing the grasses to dominate. Mowing a lawn has the same effect: it kills most weeds and so creates a turf of pure grass.

Some savanna grasses respond to grazing by growing faster – the more that animals nibble the grass, the quicker it grows back. In fact, certain

grass species can't survive without being grazed. One example is an African grass called *Andropogon greenwayi*, which makes up about half the grass in parts of the savanna that are regularly grazed. When people put up fences to keep animals away, *Andropogon greenwayi* disappears and other plants take its place.

Having a continuous haircut is no problem for grass plants, so they have little need for thorns or poisons to ward off animals. As a result, tropical grasslands are a living banquet – vast herds of plant-eating animals can gorge themselves on the fast-growing grasses, which soon grow back. In contrast, plants in tropical rainforests defend themselves against **herbivores** with an armoury of chemical weapons, such as tannin (which makes leaves indigestible) and strychnine (a lethal neurotoxin). Rainforest animals have to be much more choosy about what they eat.

Going underground

During the dry season, most tropical grasses allow their blades and flowers to wither, dry out and die. But the grass plants themselves do not die – they store their food reserves underground in swollen roots or stems, which

Above: The tussock grasses (bunch grasses) of northern Australia grow in large clumps called tussocks, giving the ground a lumpy appearance.

Flame lilies get through Africa's dry season by storing food in an underground swelling called a tuber. They bloom in the wet season, using long, twining leaves to crawl up through the grass and reach the light.

stay inactive until the next wet season. These underground parts have tiny buds, ready to sprout into action when the rains return. Other tropical grassland plants, such as orchids and lilies, use the same trick. Like hibernating animals, all these plants survive the harsh weather by conserving their energy, doing very little and hiding. In West African savannas, the total weight of plant matter underground may be up to four times as much as that above the surface. All this hidden material provides food for armies of burrowing animals, especially termites, worms and rodents.

Not all grasses stop growing in the dry season, though. Some species continue growing, but much more slowly. These grasses are common in places that have occasional

Pointless pollen

Like other flowering plants, grasses produce flowers, which allow them to reproduce sexually. The male parts of flowers make a windblown dust called pollen, while the female parts produce sticky receptors to catch pollen. When pollen lands on the female part of a flower, the male and female sex cells join and a seed forms. Or at least that's what usually happens – but some grasses have abandoned the sexual process. They still go to the trouble of producing flowers and pollen, but instead of reproducing sexually they clone themselves at the last minute, making seeds that grow into carbon copies of the single parent.

Scientists think the grasses that reproduce this way do so because it preserves a very successful combination of genes. When organisms reproduce sexually, genes from the parents mix together. This results in varied offspring, each with a unique set of genes and unique strengths. However, it also scrambles the parental genes like decks of cards being shuffled, breaking up useful combinations.

Below: Madagascar is home to the bizarre elephant's-foot plant, so named because its bloated stem looks like a severed elephant's foot that has sprouted flowers.

Acacia trees develop a flat canopy because giraffes and other animals nibble them from below.

bursts of rain in the middle of the dry season. By keeping a few tiny shoots alive above ground, they are ready to spring to life before other plants when conditions improve.

Hiding underground is not just a good way of surviving dry weather – it's also an excellent defence against the wildfires that sweep across tropical grasslands every dry season. Like grazing, fire can help grass plants. For one thing, it kills tree seedlings, stopping them from growing big enough to shade out the grass. It also clears the ground of debris, allowing new shoots to emerge into full sunlight as soon as they break the surface.

Year after year

In temperate countries, such as North America, many plants are **annuals**. Annual plants don't try to survive the harsh winters. Instead, they simply die after scattering their seeds and leave the seeds to grow into new plants the next year.

In tropical grasslands, there are very few annual plants. Most are **perennials** – plants that carry on growing year after year. Perennials have one big advantage over annuals: by storing food reserves, they can spring to life more quickly in the growing season. In contrast, plants that grow from seeds start off small and take weeks to grow large. When the wet season begins, there is a race to grow as quickly as possible to colonize the bare ground. Perennials are quickest. Helped by the warmth and the intense sunshine, they cover the ground in days. Late starters risk being left in the shade, without enough sunlight to grow properly.

Another strategy that helps grass plants take over quickly is the way they reproduce. Although tropical grasses can reproduce by seed, they rely much more on cloning themselves. Instead of growing upwards, some

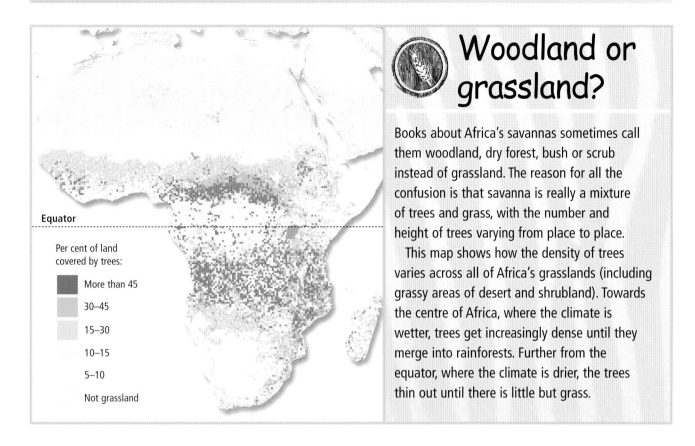

Equator

Per cent of land
covered by trees:

More than 45

30–45

15–30

10–15

5–10

Not grassland

Woodland or grassland?

Books about Africa's savannas sometimes call them woodland, dry forest, bush or scrub instead of grassland. The reason for all the confusion is that savanna is really a mixture of trees and grass, with the number and height of trees varying from place to place.

This map shows how the density of trees varies across all of Africa's grasslands (including grassy areas of desert and shrubland). Towards the centre of Africa, where the climate is wetter, trees get increasingly dense until they merge into rainforests. Further from the equator, where the climate is drier, the trees thin out until there is little but grass.

grass stems creep along the ground or grow horizontally under the surface. At a certain distance, these stems take root and produce a new tuft of shoots. The resulting clumps of grass, called tussocks, are a common sight in most tropical grasslands. This way of reproducing is much faster than making seeds and allows a single plant to colonize a large area quickly with clones of itself.

Flat tops and twisted trunks

Most tropical grasslands have at least a scattering of trees and shrubs as well as grasses. The trees are most abundant in the rainiest areas or where the soil is damp, and they gradually thin out as the grassland merges into desert or shrubland. There are also occasional thickets, especially along river banks or near water holes.

In Africa and Madagascar, most of the trees in savannas are acacias – members of the same family of plants as peas and beans. Like their relatives, acacias produce nutritious

seed pods that are full of **protein**, and much sought after by giraffes, elephants and antelope. But the seeds themselves are not always fully digested. When they pass out of the animal, they land on the ground in a heap of dung, which provides the perfect fertilizer. So, in a way, the trees pay the animals to spread their seeds and plant them.

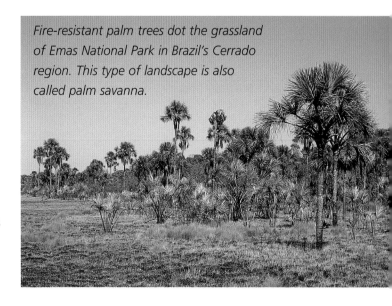

Fire-resistant palm trees dot the grassland of Emas National Park in Brazil's Cerrado region. This type of landscape is also called palm savanna.

The whistling thorn tree

If you stand next to an acacia tree in the savannas of East Africa, you might hear it whistling. The noise comes from the wind blowing through holes in swellings at the base of thorns (right), which act like tiny flutes. Thanks to the tree's musical ability, people call it the whistling thorn tree. The swollen thorns provide homes for particularly aggressive types of ants, the acacia ants. In addition to housing the ants, the tree produces sugary secretions that feed them. In return, the ants protect the tree from animals. When a giraffe tries to grab a mouthful of leaves with its tongue, the ants swarm out of their thorns and attack with vicious stings.

As young acacias grow, their sides tend to get nibbled by animals, but the centre of the plant, where the leaves and pods are out of reach, grows tall. Once this part of the tree has become too tall for even giraffes to reach, it spreads out, giving the tree its famous flat-topped appearance.

Savanna trees have to contend with the same problems as grasses – the long dry season, unpredictable rain, wildfires and hungry animals – but they overcome these problems in different ways. The baobab tree gets through the dry season by absorbing as much water as it can in the wet season and swelling in size. It also sheds its leaves and stays bare for up to nine months a year.

With deeper roots than grasses, trees can reach further underground for water. One Brazilian savanna tree has roots that grow up to 18 metres (60 feet) deep. Being able to reach deep water allows savanna trees to keep growing in the dry season, and even to flower. To conserve water, such trees often have small, leathery leaves, with fewer pores than other trees. The eucalyptus trees of Australia look like this. They are called evergreen trees because they always have leaves. However, many savanna trees shed their leaves when the dry season begins and wait for the rains to return – they are called deciduous trees.

Most savanna trees are shorter than their forest cousins, with a more twisted shape. This is especially true of Brazil's Cerrado, which is dotted with what look like gnarled and stunted little apple trees. The trees grow this way because new twigs and branches

One of the most common trees in the savannas of Zimbabwe and Botswana is the mopane tree. In the wet season its distinctive, butterfly-shaped leaves are devoured by caterpillars called mopane worms, which local people harvest for their nutty flavour.

develop each wet season, sprouting from buds hidden under the bark. In the driest parts of the Cerrado, the same plant species are so gnarled and stunted that they form shrubs rather than trees.

Fire is less of a problem for tall trees than for grasses because their buds and leaves are out of the flames' reach. Nevertheless, savanna trees generally have thick, corky bark that protects the living tissue below from being scorched. If an intense fire burns through the bark, many trees can produce new sprouts from their roots or stumps. Of all savanna trees, the masters at surviving fire

The punishing climate makes the trees of Brazil's Cerrado grow into grotesque shapes. The fruits of this monkey-nut tree look and taste like those of its close relative the cashew-nut tree.

are the eucalyptus trees of Australia, which can sprout up from the ground year after year despite being completely burned down.

Tropical grasslands are full of life, but they are tough places to survive in. As a result, the plants do not live as long as in tropical forests. Except for baobabs, which can live for thousands of years, very few shrubs or trees last more than a few decades. The same is true of grassland animals. They lead short and stressful lives, and must contend not only with fires and droughts, but also with some of the world's deadliest **predators**.

 # What a sucker

The eucalyptus's apparently miraculous ability to survive being burnt is due to its unusual roots. Many eucalyptus trees have large root swellings called lignotubers, as well as a network of underground branches called suckers. After a fire, the tree draws on the food stored in its lignotubers and quickly produces new shoots from the suckers, which emerge from the ash-covered ground as if by magic.

Sahel and Sudanian savanna

To the south of Africa's mighty Sahara Desert is a vast belt of mostly dry tropical grassland. It forms a transition zone between sandy desert to the north and forest to the south.

Many of the Sahel's people live by travelling with cattle herds in search of fresh pasture, a way of life called nomadic pastoralism.

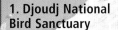

1. Djoudj National Bird Sanctuary
This wetland in the Senegal River Delta is a sanctuary for more than a million birds, including white pelicans, purple herons, African spoonbills and great egrets.

2. Senegal River
A west-flowing river on the Senegal–Mauritania border. It floods in the wet season, creating huge wetlands that many migrating birds visit. The floods also nourish rich

pasture, providing precious grazing for people's livestock.

3. Inland Niger Delta
A region of lakes and creeks formed where water from the Niger River fills wind-eroded depressions in the ground. The region dries out in droughts or severe dry seasons.

4. Niger River
Western Africa's principal river. It flows in a great arc through the Sahel and

Fact file

▲ The Sahel is a semi-arid region of grassland bordering the Sahara. The Sudanian savanna is a more lush grassland to the south of the Sahel.

▲ Only tough, drought-resistant plants, such as tussock grass and shrubby acacia trees, survive in the Sahel. Taller acacias, elephant grass and combretum trees flourish in the Sudanian savanna.

▲ The dry season lasts eight to nine months in the Sahel and five to seven months in the Sudanian savanna. Grasses wither and trees shed their leaves during the dry season.

▲ Unreliable rains make the Sahel a fragile environment, prone to becoming desert after drought or excessive grazing.

Sudanian savanna and meets the Atlantic Ocean at the Niger Delta.

5. Chad Basin National Park

Migrating birds, ostriches, red-fronted gazelles and giraffes are among the residents of this reserve in Nigeria.

6. Waza National Park

Cameroon's most famous national park hosts more than 1000 elephants – the largest concentration of the animals in the Sahel and Sudanian region.

7. Lake Chad

This shallow freshwater lake is the remains of an inland sea that has been shrinking for thousands of years. Droughts in recent decades have reduced the lake's area dramatically and turned the land around it to desert. Lake Chad is a vital source of fresh water to both people and wildlife.

8. Sahara

An enormous sandy desert that takes up almost all of northern Africa.

9. Manovo-Gounda St Floris National Park

The best-protected area of savanna in the Central African Republic, once home to African hunting dogs and black rhinos. Armed poachers have killed many of the animals and have made the park too dangerous for tourists.

10. White Nile

One of the two main tributaries of the Nile, Africa's longest river. The swamp-fringed White Nile flows through Sudan before joining the Blue Nile at Khartoum, the capital of Sudan.

11. Ethiopian Highlands

Savanna merges into lush mountain grasslands and tropical forests in the highlands of Ethiopia.

AFRICA

Sahara
8
NIGER
Lake Chad
7
Sahel
Red Sea
Nile
Khartoum
ERITREA
SUDAN
CHAD
Chad Basin National Park
5
N'Djamena
Blue Nile
ETHIOPIA
NIGERIA
6
Sudanian savanna
Abuja
Waza National Park
9
Manovo-Gounda St Floris National Park
10
Addis Ababa
White Nile
Ethiopian
11
CENTRAL AFRICAN REPUBLIC
Highlands
Niger Delta
CAMEROON
Rainforest
Bangui
Yaoundé
DEMOCRATIC REPUBLIC OF THE CONGO
UGANDA
KENYA
EQUATORIAL GUINEA
REPUBLIC OF THE CONGO
Congo basin
GABON

Clinging on

The Sahel and Sudanian savanna does not have such rich wildlife as East Africa's savanna. One reason for the difference is the drier climate, especially in the north, which makes it difficult for all but the toughest animals to survive. Another factor is hunting. In the 20th century, hunters equipped with rifles and four-wheel-drive cars killed off many animals that were once widespread here, such as lions and cheetahs. A third factor is disease – or rather the lack of it. In East and Central Africa, a disease spread by the tsetse fly made livestock farming difficult until recently, but the drier parts of northern Africa are free of the tsetse fly. As a result, herders have long been able to drive their cattle across these grasslands, causing inevitable conflict with wild animals. Even so, populations of elephants, giraffes and other large mammals survive in parts of the Sudano-Sahelian savanna, especially in the few protected reserves.

Grassland animals

For animals, grasslands are one of the richest biomes on Earth, with food covering the ground for miles on end. Yet life here is anything but easy – the animals must struggle constantly not only to find their next meal but to avoid becoming someone else's.

African elephants use their vast ears as radiators to help them lose heat. They also flap their ears wide open as a sign of anger.

Trunks have more uses than Swiss army knives. Elephants use them for smelling and touching objects, tearing up grass, stripping bark and leaves off trees, squirting water, throwing dust and scratching itchy skin. They also serve as trumpets for making sound and as snorkels for breathing underwater.

Weaver birds

Grass has other uses besides being food. Mice use it to line their nests, and lions use it for cover while stalking prey, for instance. But perhaps the most imaginative use of grass is that shown by weaver birds. Members of this bird family weave strips of leaves and grass into elaborate nests high in savanna trees. Hanging upside down by their feet, they use their tiny beaks to knot the strips together with incredible dexterity. Some species even add a trumpet-shaped entrance tube. In southern Africa, sociable weavers transform trees into huge colonies, with hundreds of nests joined together. Only the males build nests. The females select their partners by the quality of their craftsmanship.

Tropical grasslands are home to the biggest and most spectacular land animals on Earth. In a brief drive across Kenya's Masai Mara National Reserve, it takes a matter of minutes to spot elephants, giraffes, lions, hippos and cheetahs, not to mention vast herds of zebras and wildebeest, and a handful of different gazelle species. Most of these animals belong to a group that scientists call **ungulates** – the hoofed **mammals**.

On the hoof

An ungulate is an animal that has hooves and eats plants. Ungulates dominate many of the world's grasslands, both temperate and tropical, because they are experts at digesting grass. For many animals, ourselves included, grass is a poor quality food. Its cells have a tough outer coating made of a substance called cellulose, which is tricky to digest. Many grasses also contain crystals of silica (sand), which scratch an animal's teeth and wear them down. Ungulates have several ways of getting around these problems.

The teeth and jaws of ungulates work like grinders, crushing grass so powerfully that the cells split open, releasing the nutrients inside. Powerful cheek muscles move the lower jaw

sideways, scraping the flat-topped teeth across each other to mash up the grass caught in between. Silica is no problem because ungulate teeth have huge crowns that continually grow as they wear away.

The digestive system of most ungulates contains billions of cellulose-digesting bacteria. In some ungulates, including wildebeest and gazelles, these bacteria live in a stomach chamber called a rumen; such animals are called **ruminants**. Swallowed food sits in the rumen for up to four days while the bacteria get to work on it. Then the animal brings the rotting grass back up to its mouth to chew it a second time. Ruminants have a very efficient digestive system, but it works

Strange diets

Although ungulates are basically plant eaters, a few sometimes eat animals to supplement their diet. Small antelope, such as duikers, eat birds when they can catch them. Warthogs – ugly relatives of farmyard pigs – eat insects, birds, mice, frogs, worms, beetles, rotten meat and elephant dung, as well as plant food. Giraffes often eat bones (above) left by scavengers, though doing so occasionally gives them fatal food poisoning.

slowly and they can't take in huge amounts of food. As a result, such animals are fussy about what plants they eat, choosing only the youngest, most nutritious shoots.

Other ungulates have cellulose-digesting bacteria in the rear part of their digestive system. Zebras, elephants and rhinoceroses all digest food this way. It's quicker but less efficient than rumination, so they have to take in more food to compensate. These animals can survive on the tougher or older bits of grass, but they have to eat huge amounts of it. Elephants can even eat bark.

Living together

One of the reasons that many different ungulate species can coexist in a savanna is that they feed on different types of plant matter. In Africa, zebras and wildebeest often

Left: Impalas are ruminants, preferring the most tender grasses and herbs. The elegant, lyre-shaped horns of this animal identify him as a male.

live in mixed herds. While the zebras feed on the rough tops of grass plants, the wildebeest eat the small shoots that the zebras have exposed. It doesn't always work out so fairly, however. Wildebeest are often followed by small, nimble gazelles that use their narrow muzzles to steal the shoots uncovered where the ground is trampled. Rather than shooing these intruders away, the wildebeest simply move on to where the grazing is better.

Herbivores can be just as violent as carnivores, especially when fighting over mates. Male plains zebras kick and bite each other viciously in their battles over females.

Some ungulates are **browsers** rather than grazers: instead of eating grass, they nibble leaves or berries from the savanna trees. As with grazers, different browsers prefer different bits of the same tree. Giraffes browse among the highest branches, using their incredibly long and flexible tongue to reach between thorns and pluck off leaves. Long-necked antelope called gerenuks stand on their back legs to reach medium-height leaves, while small antelope such as dik-diks browse near ground level. Because trees have much deeper roots than grass, they can reach deeper water and continue growing in the dry season. This is an advantage for browsers. While grazers have to move away in the dry season to search for fresh pasture, browsers can stay put. They even survive in drier places such as shrublands and deserts.

Moving on

One of the biggest challenges that grassland animals face is the dry season. Browsers can get by on shrubs and trees, but grazers are not so lucky – their main source of food shrivels up and disappears. In South America, white-tailed deer and pampas deer stay near water holes or rivers, surviving on a mixture of grazing and browsing. They live in small herds, which makes the food last longer. In northern Australia, wallabies and kangaroos also survive on a mixed diet. Rather than forming herds, they spread out and live singly, again reducing competition for food. In Africa, however, there are vast herds of animals that eat only grass. They have no option but to migrate.

A life of danger

Grassland herbivores live a life of constant danger – especially in East Africa, where they share the savannas with many of the world's deadliest carnivores. To survive, the herbivores need ways of giving the predators a run for their money.

One defensive strategy is speed. Most ungulates are quick on their feet, especially antelope, gazelles and zebras, which can reach speeds of 64–80 km/h (40–50 mph). Even a newborn antelope can get to its feet and run within about 15 minutes of birth. The fastest savanna ungulates can outrun most predators, though they cannot match the speed of their temperate-grassland cousins the saiga and pronghorn, among the fastest land animals on Earth. Some antelope also try to confuse their pursuers by dodging randomly or making sudden, stiff-legged leaps into the air while running. The springbok earned its name from its spectacular defensive leaps, which can reach 3.5 metres (11.5 ft) high. Australia's largest native herbivores – kangaroos – also use speed to escape predators. Large kangaroos can sustain hopping speeds of more than 56 km/h (35 mph), using their heavy tails to stay balanced and aid sudden manoeuvres.

Big is best

Another strategy is size. Elephants, buffalo and rhinos are too big for most predators to overpower, though their young are much less safe. Large animals are likely to stand their ground rather than flee when threatened, and many can charge at attackers with alarming speed and ferocity. Giraffes also gain some protection from size, but lions can bring them down by driving them into broken ground where they are likely to trip. Despite their ungainly stature, giraffes can run at 56 km/h (35 mph), though their graceful strides give the appearance of moving in slow motion.

The migration

One of the world's most spectacular natural events is the migration of wildebeest in East Africa – biologists simply call it 'the migration'. Every year, herds of up to 1.5 million wildebeest leave the south-east of the Serengeti National Park in Tanzania as the dry season begins. Accompanied by zebras and gazelles, they travel north-west towards Lake Victoria, then north into Kenya's Masai Mara National Reserve, where there is permanent water and lush grass. They face many dangers on this perilous journey, such as river crossings where hundreds fall prey to crocodiles. When the rains return, the wildebeest head south again, braving the rivers once more to return to their starting point. Savanna animals also migrate in other parts of Africa, though on a smaller scale. In the west of Africa's Sahel grasslands, for instance, elephant herds travel in a giant circle that takes in wetlands and lakes when the dry season is at its worst.

There is something puzzling about the great migrations in Africa. In the Masai Mara, there is good grazing all year round, so why don't the animals simply stay put? Scientists have not yet solved this mystery, but there seem to be several factors involved. One is the large number of big cats and hyenas in the Masai Mara. These big predators tend to stay in one territory rather than migrate, because their babies cannot walk easily (unlike baby wildebeest and elephants, which can walk within hours of birth). So although the Masai Mara has good grazing, the danger of being killed by a predator there is much higher. Another factor is food

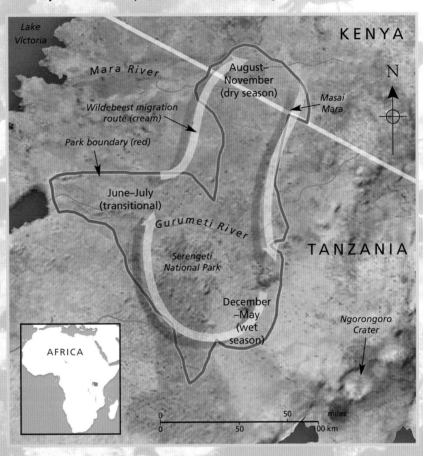

quality. The grass in the Masai Mara contains very little of the mineral phosphorus, which is vital for healthy bones. During the dry season, the wildebeest develop a phosphorus deficiency, but this disappears when they return to the mineral-rich grasslands in the south-east of the Serengeti.

Swarming locusts

Just like wildebeest, some plant-eating insects make mass migrations to find fresh grazing. Certain types of locusts form swarms so vast that they can look like dust storms. A single swarm may contain as many as 10,000 million locusts – enough to strip farmland bare in a matter of minutes, causing a famine.

Locusts are normally solitary insects, coloured green or yellow for camouflage. But if they become crowded together and their food runs out, something strange happens. They lay eggs as normal, but the hatchlings grow into large-winged, black-and-yellow locusts that cluster together before flying off in a swarm. Most swarms form on the dry fringes of the savanna, where the rains are unreliable and the food supply erratic. Although the swarms try to reach greener parts of the savanna, they sometimes get blown off course by the wind and drown at sea. In 1869 a swarm of African locusts was blown all the way to England.

Safety in numbers

Animals that live in herds, flocks or family groups benefit from safety in numbers. With so many eyes and ears on the alert for danger, predators find it much harder to sneak up and take them by surprise. Gazelles warn one another of danger by flashing their white tails and leaping. Like many herbivores, but unlike most predators, they have eyes positioned on the sides of the head. This arrangement gives a very wide field of view, the better to spot an approaching predator. Meerkats take turns keeping a lookout, perched on a bush or rock, while the rest of the group forage about on the ground for food. If danger threatens, the lookout barks a noisy warning, sending the whole group scurrying for cover.

Seeking sanctuary

Burrows provide a relatively safe haven for all sorts of small grassland animals, especially rodents, such as mice and rats. Their underground homes not only provide a hiding place from predators but also protect them from the sweltering midday heat of the dry season or the torrential rain of the wet season. In the llanos of Venezuela, cane mice emerge from their burrows at night to feast on grass seeds. In good years, they explode in number and wear down conspicuous runways through the grass. In Africa, naked mole rats spend their entire lives underground, feeding on roots, **bulbs** and other plant parts. Their social groups are unique among mammals – each colony has a queen that bears all the young, while the other mole rats are workers.

The baboons and patas monkeys of Africa (among the few **primates** that live in grassland rather than forest) spend the night sleeping in trees or on rocky cliffs, where most predators

Small herbivores rely on speed to outrun cheetahs, but youngsters such as this Thomson's gazelle are often too slow or clumsy to escape.

Hopping might look ungainly, but grey kangaroos can reach speeds of 55 km/h (35 mph) – nearly twice as fast as a person can sprint.

cannot reach them. At sunrise they come down to forage for food on the ground. Like most monkeys, they have excellent colour vision for finding food in daylight, but very poor night vision. In contrast, big herbivores such as zebras, which have no choice but to spend their nights on the open plains, have good night vision. They stay awake most of the night, watching nervously for lions and hyenas, which are most active in the hours of darkness. Like horses, zebras sleep in short bursts while standing up, their leg muscles locked in place to prevent their falling over.

A taste for flesh

Where herbivores are common, carnivores are never far away. The savannas of East Africa are famous for the wide range of flesh eaters they harbour, from big cats and hyenas to vultures and birds of prey. Less spectacular, but equally important, are the insect eaters that thrive on the countless ants, termites, caterpillars and grasshoppers. In South

Meerkats give warning calls to their group when they spot predators. They use a special call for birds of prey, telling the group to sprint headlong to the nearest hole.

Long-nosed armadillos snuffle through grass and dead leaves for insects and other small animals. Oddly, their litters always consist of genetically identical offspring.

Pangolins specialize in eating ants and termites. Like armadillos, they can curl up into an armoured ball to defend themselves against predators.

America these include armadillos and giant anteaters, while pangolins and aardvarks play similar ecological roles in Africa.

Animal flesh is a very nutritious type of food – much more so than grass – but predators have to work hard to get it. Grassland herbivores are nervous and quick-witted animals, liable to bolt at the first sign

Only by working together can lions overpower animals as large as adult buffalo. A powerful bite to the throat quickly kills the animal.

of danger, and tough enough to put up a serious fight. To catch them, predators need cunning, strength, speed and perseverance.

Working together

Some hunters use teamwork to trap or overpower their prey. Prides of lions spread out during the hunt, using any cover available to creep within striking distance before making an attack. When their prey tries to escape, a few lions often stay hidden, ready to ambush animals that blunder past.

Wildebeest and zebras are among their favourite prey when lions hunt in packs, while solitary lions often kill warthogs. But, like many carnivores, lions are opportunists, willing to tackle all sorts of prey (including people) in many different situations, as well as scavenge the kills of other predators.

Hyenas are best known as scavengers, but the largest species – the spotted hyena – is also a pack hunter, able to bring down zebras and even buffalo. Spotted hyenas are also called laughing hyenas because of the eerie cackles and 'wooooo-up' calls they make to one another. They are attracted by the sound of commotion and use their sharp sense of smell to sniff out carcasses. Packs of hyenas often muscle in on leopards or cheetahs after a hunt, using strength of numbers to steal the kill. Leopards drag kills into trees to avoid this fate, while cheetahs hunt mainly during the day, when hyenas are usually resting.

Above: Spotted hyenas have immensely powerful teeth and jaws. They can crush and eat all but the largest bones and chew their way though thick hides.

 # Fatal footwork

Despite its elegant appearance and sedate manner, the secretary bird is a vicious killer. Its main weapons are heavy, club-like feet, which it uses to stamp the life out of mice, insects, birds and lizards. It can even dispatch poisonous snakes, using a single, well-aimed blow to shatter the spine just behind the snake's head. All but the largest items of prey are swallowed whole.

Clean-up squad

Contrary to popular belief, African vultures do not rely on leftovers from predator kills. They feed mainly on the carcasses of animals that die of sickness or old age. Typically, white-headed vultures find a carcass before any other vultures do. But soon hoards of griffon vultures such as the white-backed vulture (above) arrive, squabbling noisily. Their bald heads let them plunge deep into a carcass and come out clean. Eventually, huge lappet-faced vultures arrive to muscle their way in. It takes only a day or so for a carcass to disappear from Africa's savanna, thanks to the work of nature's clean-up squad.

Unlike the big cats, which generally bring down prey after a sudden dash, African hunting dogs chase their victims over long distances, gradually wearing them out. Small animals are torn apart and devoured in a frenzy as soon as they are caught; larger animals are often disembowelled during the chase by repeated bites to the flank and rear. Once common in Africa's savannas, hunting dogs are now very rare, possibly because of diseases spread by domestic dogs.

With its kill safely wedged in a tree, this leopard can feed without being challenged by lions or hyenas.

Lone hunters

Leopards and cheetahs usually hunt alone, using different strategies to catch their prey. Leopards hunt by stealth, hiding in trees or thickets to sneak close enough to ambush antelope and other prey. Cheetahs use speed to run down small gazelles and antelope in daylight, favouring young animals, which are slower and less nimble than adults. After

Dingoes are the top predators in Australia's grasslands. Though wild today, they are descendants of tame dogs brought to Australia by people thousands of years ago.

tripping the prey with a flick of the paw, the cheetah kills it with a suffocating bite to the neck – a technique common to all cats. Cheetahs are the fastest animals on land, capable of about 100 km/h (60 mph) on level ground, but they can sprint for only 10–30 seconds before they risk overheating.

Around the world

To most people, the word *savanna* conjures up images of vast herds of hoofed mammals roaming over grassy plains, ever watchful for lions, hyenas and other big predators. In East Africa, that's a fairly accurate image, but not all tropical grasslands are like that. Compared to the savannas of Africa, South America's tropical grasslands seem almost devoid of large animals. Africa has around 91 different ungulate species, but South America has just 21, and only 3 of those live primarily in tropical grasslands. Australia has no native ungulates. Instead, wallabies and kangaroos are the main plant-eaters in the savanna.

The reasons for these differences are complicated. According to evidence from fossils, South America's grasslands may once have been as rich in animal life as Africa's, but about 10,000 years ago many of the animals disappeared. No one knows exactly why. Perhaps people hunted them to extinction, or perhaps the climate changed and the animals couldn't adapt. Whatever the reason, the animals that were left behind were much less diverse. Today, most of the mammals that live in the llanos and Cerrado are the same species that live in South America's tropical forests. There are exceptions – such as the maned wolf, a kind of dog that looks like a fox on stilts, and the pampas deer – but they are few.

 # Tasmanian tiger

Until about 4000 years ago, Australia had its own native version of a big cat: the thylacine, or Tasmanian tiger. This strange marsupial looked like a mixture of other animals: it had the head and front legs of a wolf, hind legs more like a kangaroo's and a back covered in the stripes of a tiger. Thylacines probably died out in Australia because of competition with dingoes, but they survived on the island of Tasmania until the 20th century. Sadly, they were hunted to extinction by sheep farmers; the last captive animal died in 1930.

Ostriches (left), rheas (centre) and emus (right) live in different parts of the world but have similar grassland lifestyles. These males are all guarding nests.

Australia's story is different. The mammals of Africa, Asia and the Americas are similar because these continents were joined until recently, allowing species to spread. South America once had elephants, for instance, and its jaguar is a close cousin of Africa's big cats. Australia, however, has been separate from the rest of the world for millions of years, cut adrift like Noah's ark with a unique collection of **marsupials** (mammals with pouches). Another difference is that Australia has no large predators, apart from the ones that people have introduced. The nearest thing to a lion in Australia is the dingo – a wild dog descended from tame dogs brought to Australia by Aborigines.

Despite the differences, there are some striking similarities in the animal life of the world's major tropical grasslands. One similarity is the presence of large flightless birds: ostriches in Africa, emus in Australia and rheas in South America. All three have lost the power of flight and have long, powerful legs for sprinting across the open terrain; ostriches can reach 60 km/h (37 mph) when just a month old.

Ostriches, rheas and emus share some surprisingly similar patterns of behaviour.

In all three species, the male mates with several females, incubates their eggs in a communal nest and looks after the young when they hatch. All three species live in flocks for protection from predators, and their diets are similar, consisting mainly of plants and seeds and supplemented by insects such as grasshoppers. Ostriches – the world's largest birds – also eat lizards and turtles.

Just why these birds are so similar is a matter of hot debate. Some scientists think they evolved along similar lines because they live in similar environments – a process called convergent evolution. However, other scientists think the birds inherited these traits from a common ancestor that lived millions of years ago, when the Earth's continents were joined in one landmass.

Grassland insects

Another similarity among the world's tropical grasslands is their insect life. The biggest grass-eaters in savannas are mammals, but the animals that eat the most grass are much smaller. Hordes of grasshoppers and ants scurry and hop through the turf, while caterpillars munch the leaves and armies of termites collect dead plant litter.

Termite mounds provide handy lookout towers for baboons and other animals. Deep inside, the grotesquely enlarged queen (inset) is busy laying eggs.

Dung beetles

Dung beetles clear up fresh manure from tropical grasslands almost as fast as it appears. Working quickly while the dung is still soft and pliable, they form it into balls and roll these away to their burrows. Once safely underground, the beetles lay eggs in the dung balls, and the grubs develop inside them. Some dung beetles don't go to the trouble of making dung balls and

rolling them away; instead they dig a burrow right under the main dung heap. One Australian species does not even dig burrows – it has evolved into a parasite that lives in the large intestines of wallabies.

Termites play the role of recyclers. They consume a quarter to a third of the dead plant matter in tropical grasslands, though they don't always eat this directly. The fungus-growing termites carry litter deep into their complex nests and use it to grow fungi, which members of the colony then eat. Like ants, termites are social insects. A colony may contain many thousands of individuals, but all the eggs are laid by a single queen. A queen termite can lay thousands of eggs a day and grow as large as a person's finger – so large that she is unable to move. In many savannas, the termites build spectacular, towering mounds that dot the landscape, forming so-called termite savannas. Within the mound, the temperature and humidity are remarkably constant, providing the perfect environment for the fungus garden and developing termite larvae.

East Africa

East Africa's savannas are famous for their astonishing diversity of large mammals and for the spectacular mass migrations of wildebeest, zebras and other herbivores.

Mount Kilimanjaro's snowcapped peak dominates the skyline over Kenya's Amboseli National Park.

Ngorongoro Crater

Ngorongoro Crater is one of the wonders of the natural world – visitors sometimes compare it to Noah's ark. Packed into this 20-km-wide (12-mile-wide) volcanic crater is just about every large mammal species to be found in East Africa's savannas, including lions, hyenas, elephants, wildebeest, zebras and rhinos. The crater even has hippo-filled water holes and its own soda lake,

complete with thousands of pink flamingos. Many of the animals stay year round, but others come only in the dry season, attracted by permanent water on the crater floor. Even without wildlife, Ngorongoro would be amazing. Surrounding the central grassy plain is a 600-metre-high (2000-ft-high) crater wall, covered in cloud forest. Visitors drive up and over the jungly rim before descending into the sun-baked interior.

Fact file

▲ Most of East Africa is savanna, but there are also large areas of treeless grassland, shrubland, tropical forest, mountains and lakes.

▲ There are two rainy seasons in East Africa: a long one between March and June, and a shorter one between October and December.

▲ Kenya and Tanzania rely heavily on income from tourists visiting their national parks. Kenya alone has more than thirty national parks and reserves.

▲ Poaching nearly wiped out East Africa's elephant and rhino populations in the 20th century. Even today, anti-poaching patrols in some parks are authorized to shoot and kill poachers.

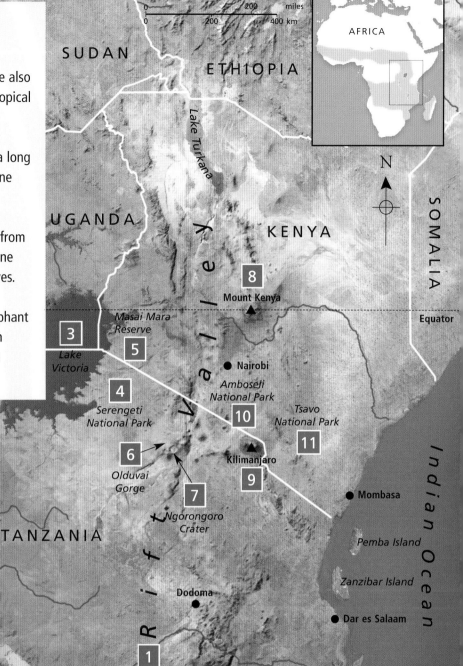

1. Great Rift Valley
A massive depression in the Earth's surface, formed by gradual separation of the African and Arabian landmasses. It extends from Jordan in the Middle East to Mozambique in Africa, where its east and west branches average 45–65 km (30–40 miles) wide.

2. Lake Tanganyika
In the western branch of the Great Rift Valley is the world's longest freshwater lake. It is also the world's second deepest lake, after Lake Baikal in Russia.

3. Lake Victoria
The world's second largest lake, and Africa's largest, occupies a shallow basin between the two branches of the Great Rift Valley. The region around Lake Victoria is one of the most densely populated parts of Africa.

4. Serengeti National Park
Tanzania's most famous national park, some 15,000 sq km (6000 sq miles) in area. Its almost treeless grassy plains are inhabited by millions of wildebeest and zebras.

5. Masai Mara National Reserve
This Kenyan reserve is joined to Tanzania's Serengeti. Packed with lions, it is one of Africa's top tourist attractions.

6. Olduvai Gorge
An archaeological site in the Serengeti plains where footprints and fossils of ancient hominids (ancestors of the human race) have been found.

7. Ngorongoro Crater
A massive volcanic crater in Tanzania, rich in savanna wildlife and rimmed by cloud forest. Protected as a world heritage site, a biosphere reserve and a Tanzanian national park.

8. Mount Kenya
An extinct volcano in the Kenyan highlands, 5199 metres (17,058 ft) high, where giant lobelias, groundsel trees and other unusual plants grow.

9. Kilimanjaro
At 5895 metres (19,340 ft), this extinct volcano is Africa's highest mountain and one of the only places in Africa that gets snow.

10. Amboseli National Park
Kenya's second most popular park after the Masai Mara. Huge herds of elephants survive here, but poachers have wiped out all the rhinos.

11. Tsavo National Park
Kenya's largest national park, at around 20,000 sq km (8000 sq miles) in area, or the size of Wales. The region was once home to the 'Tsavo man eaters', a pair of male lions that ate dozens of railway workers in 1898.

People and grasslands

Tropical grasslands were the cradle of our species and shaped our evolution. Today the relationship is reversed – we are re-shaping the world's biomes and changing tropical grasslands beyond recognition.

In 1976, **palaeontologist** Andrew Hill made a remarkable discovery at Laetoli in the Serengeti plains of Tanzania. After a long day of fossil hunting, Hill and his colleagues were amusing themselves by flinging elephant dung at one another. As Hill dived onto the ground to avoid a particularly well-aimed lump, he found himself staring at fossilized animal tracks on the ground. The discovery was a major breakthrough, but it was nothing compared to what Hill's colleagues found under the footprints. When geochemist Paul Abell quarried out a section of rhino tracks, he saw two new sets of prints underneath. These footprints, some 3.6 million years old, were unmistakably the tracks of a pair of **hominids** – apes that walked on two legs, just as humans do.

Origins

The Laetoli footprints are one of the oldest pieces of evidence suggesting that our two-legged ancestors originated in the savannas of Africa, perhaps 4 or 5 million years ago.

The 3.6-million-year-old Laetoli footprints were made by two hominids walking side by side. A third individual also seems to have walked in the larger footprints.

Today, humans are the only members of the great ape family that walk on two legs habitually. Chimps and gibbons occasionally stand and walk a few paces, but the skill has limited use in their forest habitats. Hominids, in contrast, evolved the ability to stride for miles across a more open landscape. Their legs became straighter, their toes shrank and their skulls changed shape to balance on an upright spine.

The evolution of two-legged walking, or bipedalism, seems to have been linked to a change in the African environment. About 5 million years ago, savannas were spreading throughout tropical Africa because the Earth's climate was growing cooler and drier.

The Aborigines of northern Australia harvest food from the wild, a way of life called hunter-gathering. Unlike hunter-gatherers in rainforests or deserts, however, they also use fire to manage the savanna landscape.

As the forests dwindled in size, our tree-dwelling ancestors evolved better ways of getting about on the ground.

In addition to evolving a new posture, hominids lost most of the body hair that had covered their ape-like predecessors, and they evolved a far more efficient sweating system. These two changes allowed hominids to stay active during the heat of the day in the open savanna environment, exposed to the tropical sun. The price they paid for their advanced cooling system was a continual need for water – our ancestors probably never strayed very far from rivers or water holes.

Adjusting to life on the savanna not only affected our ancestors' bodies, it also changed their diet. Forest foods such as fruit and nuts became harder to find, while roots, grass seeds and meat became more important. Having no natural weapons for killing large prey, the early hominids probably got much of their meat by scavenging in groups. However, with their hands free to make tools, they soon began making hunting weapons, such as simple knives made from chipped rocks and spears made from sharpened sticks.

Humans have now spread throughout the world's biomes, yet we retain our tropical biology. Instead of evolving blubber or fur in colder climates, for instance, we built houses and made clothes to recreate a tropical microclimate. One of the few evolutionary changes caused by our spread to new biomes was the development of paler skin, helping us to make vitamin D in weak sunlight.

 # Two legs or four?

Why tree-dwelling apes should evolve into two-legged (bipedal) rather than four-legged walkers is a matter of debate. After all, other savanna primates, such as baboons and patas monkeys, manage perfectly well on all fours. Some scientists think bipedalism evolved because the upright posture exposed less of the body to the midday sun, helping hominids avoid overheating when out in the open. Others think the main advantage was the ability to look over the grass and scan the horizon for predators or prey. Or, perhaps, bipedalism enabled our ancestors to carry their offspring and so follow the herds of migrating herbivores – something other predators, such as lions, cannot do. Whatever the reason, bipedalism had a very important consequence: it freed the hominids' hands, allowing them to make and use tools.

The Maasai people of East Africa live by herding cattle across the savanna. Songs and dances like this one are an important part of Maasai culture.

The modern world

Human culture has changed beyond recognition since our hominid ancestors first conquered the savanna. The development of language, greater intelligence and complex societies have had such far-reaching consequences that all the world's people now live in very different ways from our hominid ancestors. However, we can get clues about how people may have lived in the distant past from the way some modern people survive in tropical grasslands, using only natural resources and knowledge handed down over the generations.

Hunter-gatherers

Before the spread of agriculture and the domestication of animals, most of the world's people were **hunter-gatherers** – they lived off food collected from the wild. Today, very few people live as hunter-gatherers in tropical grasslands, but one exception is the Aboriginal people of Australia.

The Aborigines' way of life is changing fast, but many still collect wild foods in remote parts of Australia, including the tropical grasslands of the north. The bulk of their diet comes from plant foods, such as wild roots and grass seeds, which women grind into flour. Insect grubs and other small animals provide a valuable source of protein, supplemented by meat from larger animals caught in traps or hunted. A traditional hunting technique is the use of fire to smoke out wallabies and other large prey from thickets. Native mammals were never kept as livestock, probably because, unlike cattle or goats, marsupials do not usually form herds.

Despite the apparent simplicity of their hunter-gatherer lifestyle, Aborigines manage the landscape in a careful and deliberate manner, using fire to clear scrub and keep the savanna open. In recent times, European ranchers have claimed much of Australia's savanna for their cattle, and fires are now much less frequent. As a result, woody vegetation has begun to reclaim the land, turning the ancient savanna into forest.

The relationship between fire, people and grasslands is an ancient one. People have lived in tropical grasslands for millennia and used fire for just as long. Many savannas that we consider wild are probably semi-natural, like the savannas of Australia.

in search of recent rains and fresh grazing, so pastoralists must stay on the move to keep their cattle fed. The Fulani people of West Africa travel constantly and never settle down. The Maasai people of East Africa have permanent homes but take their herds far away in the dry season. Besides providing meat, their animals provide milk or blood – renewable sources of food and liquid that can be taken without killing the animals.

In southern parts of the Sudanian savanna, people grow crops as well as herd animals. However, in the drier Sahel to the north, the rains are not sufficiently reliable for crop cultivation – the only way to survive off the land is by nomadic pastoralism.

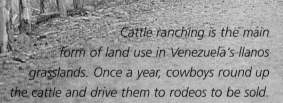

Cattle ranching is the main form of land use in Venezuela's llanos grasslands. Once a year, cowboys round up the cattle and drive them to rodeos to be sold.

Nomads and herders

In contrast to the Aborigines, the savanna-dwelling peoples of Africa live mostly by travelling with herds of animals, a way of life called nomadic pastoralism. Just as wild herbivores must migrate across the savanna

Raising livestock, especially cattle, is the main form of land use in savannas throughout the world. In South America, Australia and parts of Africa, cattle ranching has grown into a major industry, turning what was once wild and diverse savanna into uniform pasture. The llanos are now home to an estimated 15 million cattle. Ranchers burn the grasslands regularly to release nutrients and clear trees, resulting in deforestation of woodland areas and gallery forests. Though fire has always played a part

Desertification

In recent decades, a combination of factors have made life very hard for people in the Sahel (below). Governments have tried to make people settle down in one place, but this has made it difficult for once-nomadic herders to keep their animals properly fed. At the same time, a succession of droughts has reduced the amount of grazing available and forced people to gather

around wells. In areas where people are concentrated, grasses soon disappear as the animals eat them, and trees are felled for firewood or fodder. The land becomes barren and dusty, as though swallowed by the desert. Desertification is not confined to the Sahel – it is a major problem in other arid places, and an international convention now exists to combat it.

in savanna ecology, scientists believe its use is on the increase in many parts of the world, with damaging effects on the wildlife.

Cultivation of crops is also on the increase in savannas, though the harsh dry season makes this more difficult than ranching. In wet parts of the llanos, hundreds of thousands of hectares of grassland have been

Soybean fields near Goiás, central Brazil. Irrigated crops such as this one have taken the place of wild savannas throughout much of the Cerrado.

converted to corn and rice plantations. In recent years, Brazil's Cerrado has undergone an even more remarkable transformation as vast plantations of soybeans, corn and irrigated rice have appeared.

People versus animals

The impact of people on savanna wildlife is nowhere clearer than in Africa. Famous for its fearsome predators and giant herbivores, Africa's savanna is now mostly devoid of large wild mammals, except for pockets of

To protect elephants from poaching, many countries have banned trade in ivory. In Kenya, stockpiles of poached elephant tusks and rhino horns are burned to help enforce the ban.

land protected as national parks. Outside the parks, the human population is growing, roads and towns are dividing the landscape into islands of wilderness and domestic herds are replacing wild ones. Tropical diseases that affect cattle (such as trypanosomiasis, which is spread by tsetse flies) have been eradicated from many areas, allowing pastoralists to encroach on untamed parts of the savanna.

Inevitably, people and wild animals come into conflict. Livestock eat the same plants as wild herbivores, competing with them for food. And herders must protect their stock – as well as themselves – from predators, by

whatever means necessary; in some parts of Africa, killing a lion is still regarded as a test of manhood. The 20th century also saw a disturbing rise in poaching, especially of elephants for **ivory** and rhinos for their horns.

Despite the pressures confronting Africa's wildlife, the future is not entirely bleak. In recent times, people have begun to realize that one good way to protect wildlife is to make money from it, and a new industry is on the rise: ecotourism.

 # Rhino poaching

Between 1970 and the 1990s, Africa's black rhino population plummeted from an estimated 100,000 to fewer than 3000. The cause of the decline was poaching. Rhino horn is a prized ingredient in traditional Chinese medicines for impotence, and it is in even more demand in Yemen and Oman, where daggers with rhino horn handles are worn by men as a status symbol. With the fall in rhino numbers, the value of their horns on the black market soared from £16 a kilogram to more than £900, making poaching all the

more lucrative. Today, nearly all Africa's remaining black rhinos live in fenced reserves with armed guards, and many are dehorned for their own protection (above).

Northern Australia

Savanna covers a great area of northern Australia, sandwiched between tropical forests in the north and desert in the continent's interior.

 Fact file

▲ Trees in Australia's savanna include eucalyptuses, acacias, baobabs and kakadu plum trees.

▲ Eucalyptus species such as Darwin's woollybutt and Darwin's stringy-bark are often hollowed out by termites. Australians use the hollow branches to make musical instruments called didgeridoos.

▲ Tree cover decreases from north to south with the increasingly dry climate.

▲ Resident marsupials include kangaroos, wallaroos, wallabies, bilbies, quolls and long-tailed planigales – the world's smallest marsupials (*see Australian Wildlife website; address on p. 63*).

▲ The main grass in wet areas is monsoon tallgrass. Drier areas are dominated by Mitchell grass, which grows in tussocks. A Mitchell grass plant can live for thirty years.

▲ Termite mounds up to 6 metres (20 ft) tall dot much of the landscape.

| 0 | | 250 | | miles |
| 0 | 250 | | 500 | km |

Indian Ocean Eighty-Mile Beach WESTERN AUSTRALIA

Above: Bungle Bungle Range rocks were formed by sediment settling in layers millions of years ago. Forces beneath Earth's crust then lifted the rocks, as wind and water wore them down into these shapes.

1. Kimberley Plateau
A rugged sandstone plateau, covered by savanna and dissected by numerous gorges and ridges. Torrential rains in the wet season fill the temporary rivers, causing flash floods.

2. Bungle Bungle Range
A magnificent range of rocky hills that resemble giant, striped beehives.

3. Tanami Desert
Grasslands peter out in this arid part of the outback, leaving sandy plains with scattered clumps of spinifex grass and saltbush shrubs.

4. Cattle ranches
Cattle ranching is the main form of land use in northern Australia's grasslands.

5. Arnhem Land
A largely unspoilt wilderness containing eucalyptus forest, savanna and patches of rainforest and wetland. Arnhem Land provides a refuge for animals found nowhere else, such as the black wallaroo, the Earth's smallest kangaroo.

6. Barkly Tableland
A region of rolling grassy hills used as pasture by cattle ranchers.

7. Gulf of Carpentaria
Surrounding this enormous bay is a mixture of woody savanna, eucalyptus forest, sandstone cliffs and saline flats. The region is battered by monsoon rains every summer.

8. Cape York Peninsula
Australia's northern-most tip, sparsely populated except for Aboriginal reserves on the coast and cattle ranches.

9. Queensland rainforest
A small strip of dense tropical rainforest flourishes on the wet coast of Queensland.

10. Great Basalt Wall
A unique rock feature in the Queensland highlands, formed by a lava flow. Walls of basalt rock surround pockets of savanna. Cattle cannot climb the wall to reach the savanna, so native wildlife can graze without competing with livestock.

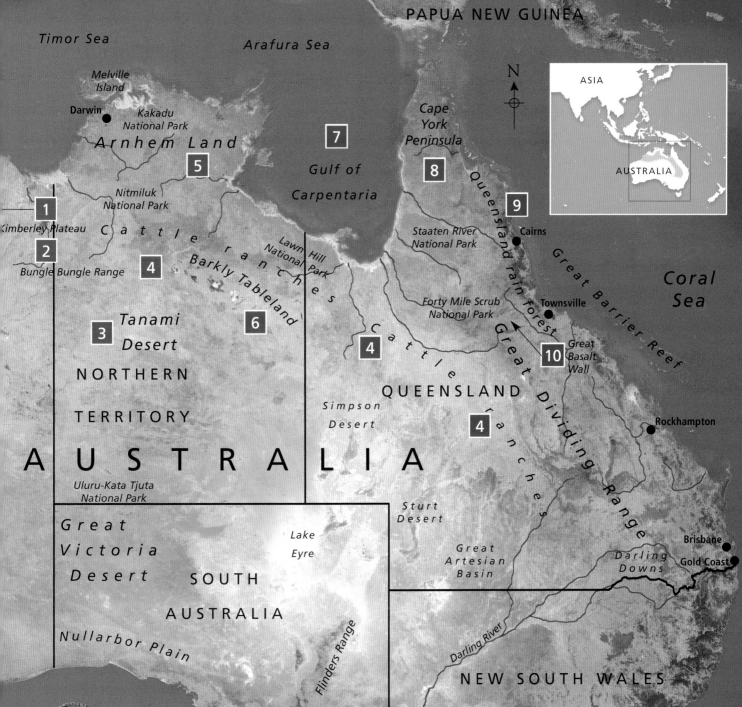

PAPUA NEW GUINEA

Timor Sea

Arafura Sea

Melville
Island

Darwin ●

Kakadu
National Park

Arnhem Land

5

7

Cape
York
Peninsula

8

Gulf of
Carpentaria

N

ASIA

AUSTRALIA

1

Nitmiluk
National Park

Cattle ranches

Kimberley Plateau

2

Barkly Tableland

Lawn Hill
National Park

9

Staaten River
National Park

Cairns ●

Queensland rain forest

Great Barrier Reef

Coral
Sea

Bungle Bungle Range

4

3

Tanami
Desert

6

Forty Mile Scrub
National Park

4

Townsville ●

Great
Basalt
Wall

10

Great Dividing Range

NORTHERN

TERRITORY

QUEENSLAND

Simpson
Desert

ranches

4

Rockhampton ●

A U S T R A L I A

Uluru-Kata Tjuta
National Park

Great
Victoria
Desert

SOUTH

AUSTRALIA

Nullarbor Plain

Lake
Eyre

Sturt
Desert

Great
Artesian
Basin

Darling
Downs

Brisbane ●
Gold Coast ●

Flinders Range

Darling River

NEW SOUTH WALES

 Life in the pouch

Marsupials raise their offspring in a very different way from other mammals. A mother kangaroo gives birth when its baby is about 1 cm (half an inch) long. The newborn youngster is blind, furless and has no hind legs. Using its relatively strong forelimbs, it climbs through the mother's fur and into a pouch, where it stays for up to eleven months, suckling on a teat. After several weeks in the pouch, the young kangaroo (called a joey) is big enough to peer outside and hop out from time to time.

The future

The world's tropical grasslands will continue changing in the future, and much of their wildlife may die out. Yet the grasslands themselves are at little risk of disappearing – if anything, they are spreading.

Confined mostly to the developing world, where the human population is growing most rapidly, the world's tropical grasslands are under threat. Agriculture, industry, pollution and urbanization are all playing a part in their transformation. Some areas have turned into bland farmland, others have become desert and many are losing their native plants and animals.

Ecotourism

In Africa, the best hope for conserving savanna wildlife perhaps lies in ecotourism. Kenya's national parks and game reserves are the envy of the world. Every year, around a million tourists visit them hoping to catch a glimpse of the 'big five': lions, elephants, rhinos, buffalo and leopards. Tourism brings around £250 million annually into Kenya, helping to fund the national parks and giving the government good reason to protect them. Tanzania earns a similar amount, while South Africa takes over £1000 million from tourists each year, mostly from ecotourism. Zambia, Zimbabwe, Madagascar and Botswana also

Safari minibuses sometimes outnumber elephants in parts of Kenya's Amboseli National Park. Many park animals are now used to vehicles and ignore them.

Though amusing to watch, baboons can be dangerous if they get too close. They often invade cars, campsites and tourist lodges in search of easy pickings.

traditional ebony carvings made by the Makonde people, unaware that the trade is killing off the African blackwood tree.

A changing biome

Tropical grasslands are one of the youngest biomes. Since they formed some 20 million years ago, they have fluctuated with changes in the Earth's climate, taking territory from forests in dry periods and reverting to forest in wetter times. Like temperate grasslands, tropical grasslands thrive on conflict and change – they flourish in areas that are periodically disturbed, either by fire, people, animals or extremes of climate.

In some parts of the world, large areas of savanna have existed for thousands of years purely because of human interference. The western part of Madagascar and nearly all of India, for instance, would probably be covered in seasonal tropical forest if they

have ecotourist industries, though those of Madagascar and Zimbabwe have suffered in recent years due to political unrest.

For the most part, tourists do little damage to the savanna **ecosystem**, but they do have an impact. In Kenya's Masai Mara, there are so many jeeps and minibuses following cheetahs that these big cats now find it difficult to hunt in daylight. Baboons and vervet monkeys have become so accustomed to food handouts that they leap on cars and intimidate campers. In the shops and markets, tourists haggle eagerly over the

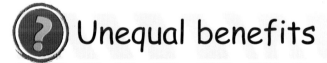

? Unequal benefits

Tourism conserves wildlife most effectively when the profits it generates end up in the hands of the local people. If locals can see the economic benefits of wild animals, they are more willing to help protect them. In Kenya, however, things have not always worked out this way. Most of the national parks and tourist lodges are run by people belonging to Kenya's Kikuyu community. In the past, the Kikuyu pocketed the profits of tourism, while the Maasai people – in whose homeland the parks are established – got next to nothing. Worse still, the Maasai's grazing rights were restricted, and in some cases people were forcibly relocated. Today, things are improving and the Maasai now earn a share of the profits.

When tropical forests are cut down, grasslands grow in their place. Cattle ranchers have turned large parts of the Amazon rainforest into pasture this way.

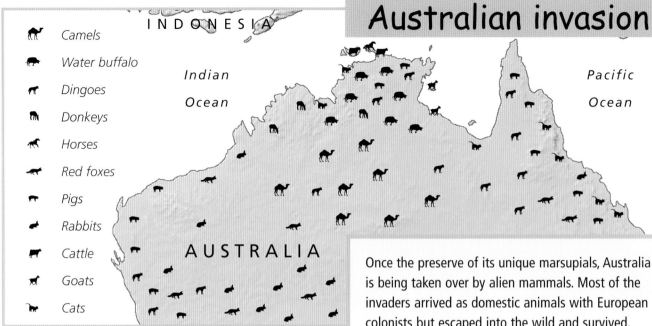

🐫	Camels
🐃	Water buffalo
🐕	Dingoes
🐴	Donkeys
🐎	Horses
🦊	Red foxes
🐗	Pigs
🐇	Rabbits
🐄	Cattle
🐐	Goats
🐈	Cats

Australian invasion

Once the preserve of its unique marsupials, Australia is being taken over by alien mammals. Most of the invaders arrived as domestic animals with European colonists but escaped into the wild and survived. First on the scene was the dingo, some 50,000 years ago; it probably drove thylacines to extinction. More recent arrivals include donkeys, buffalo and camels, brought to Australia as beasts of burden; rabbits and foxes, which were introduced to be hunted; and horses, which were bred by the army. All sorts of farm animals (with the exception of sheep) have escaped into the wild, as have rats, mice and pet cats. Many of Australia's native mammals seem unable to compete with the invaders and are likely to suffer the same fate as the thylacine.

were uninhabited. The same is true of parts of South-east Asia, Africa and northern Australia. In all these places, fire, agriculture, livestock and collection of wood for fuel all help preserve a kind of artificial savanna.

Such landscapes are spreading. As tropical forests are cut down by farmers, loggers and cattle ranchers, grasslands are taking their place. In some places, the change may be irreversible. With no trees to soak up and release moisture, the climate can get drier. Humidity drops, fewer clouds form and there is no longer enough rain for forest. When it does rain, the water simply runs off the dusty ground in sheets, washing away precious soil.

Introduced species
The world's wildest tropical grasslands are becoming more uniform. Species introduced from one continent to another sometimes multiply with unexpected speed, taking over from natives. In South America's llanos, for instance, an African grass called jaragua has spread aggressively, replacing native species in huge areas. Besides disrupting the local plant life, alien grasses deprive animals of food if they are less digestible than native

grasses. In Australia, introduced mammals seem better able to survive in the wild than the native marsupials, many of which are now threatened as a result.

Global warming
If scientists are right, gases released by human activity are making the Earth's climate warmer. Such gases add to the greenhouse effect – like the panes of glass in a greenhouse, they let sunlight in but trap heat rays emitted by the sun-warmed ground.

The greenhouse effect is a natural process that has been happening for billions of years. In recent times, however, its effects seem to

Northern quolls are disappearing from Australia's tropical grasslands. Introduced foxes and cats find them easy prey, and poultry farmers regard them as vermin.

have increased, resulting in what scientists call global warming – an increase in our planet's average temperature. The main cause of global warming is thought to be the gas **carbon dioxide**, which escapes into the atmosphere when people burn fossil fuels such as wood, coal and petrol.

Global warming could force us to redraw the map of biomes. Some parts of the tropics might become drier, causing grasslands to encroach on forest. At the same time, deserts might spread at the expense of grasslands. A rise in the Earth's temperature, however, would increase the atmosphere's humidity and bring more rain to some places. Forests might then spread at the expense of grasslands, and grasslands at the expense of deserts.

There are conflicting theories as to how grasslands might respond to global warming. The raised levels of carbon dioxide in the air might stimulate grassland plants and help them to use water more efficiently, counteracting the effects of drought. Alternatively, desertification might turn grassland to dust, releasing trapped carbon in the soil and making the greenhouse effect

worse. The increasing use of fire in grasslands not only releases carbon dioxide but also ozone, another greenhouse gas. According to some estimates, fires started by people now burn as much as 75 per cent of African savanna annually, and fires in areas of tropical forest contribute even more carbon dioxide and ozone.

Whatever the future holds, it seems likely that the grassland biome, in some shape or form, is with us to stay. Perhaps tropical grasslands will move or become completely unrecognizable – but they will still exist.

Ever resourceful, baboons and hyenas sometimes profit from the expanding human population. These two are searching for leftovers in a rubbish heap at Chobe National Park in Botswana, southern Africa.

Glossary

acacia type of flowering tropical tree common in savannas

annual plant that lives for only a year or less (*see also* perennial)

arid having a very dry climate

atmosphere layer of air around the Earth

biome major division of the living world, distinguished by its climate and wildlife

browser herbivore that feeds on trees and shrubs rather than grass (*see also* grazer)

bulb kind of fattened root used by a plant for storing food

camouflage natural disguise that makes animals or plants look like their surroundings

canopy roof-like layer of treetops in a forest

carbon dioxide one of the gases in air. Animals and plants produce carbon dioxide constantly.

carnivore flesh-eating animal. Carnivore can also mean any member of the Carnivora, an order of mostly flesh-eating mammals.

climate pattern of weather that happens in one place during an average year

cloud forest lush, misty forest found on mountains in the tropics

deforestation clearing of forest, usually carried out by cutting down or burning trees

desert place where less than 250 mm (10 in) of rain falls a year

desertification process of becoming like a desert. It can happen naturally or because of human interference.

didgeridoo large bamboo or wooden trumpet-like instrument of the Australian Aborigines

dormant so inactive as to appear lifeless. Plant seeds often stay dormant until their soil gets wet.

ecosystem collection of living animals and plants that function together with their environment. Ecosystems include food chains.

equator imaginary line around the Earth, midway between the North and South Poles

eucalyptus type of plant native to Australia. Eucalyptus trees are also called gum trees.

evaporate to turn into gas. When water evaporates, it becomes water vapour, an invisible part of the air.

evolve to change gradually over many generations. All the world's species have formed through evolution.

gallery forest strip of forest along a riverbank

grazer herbivore that mainly eats grass (*see also* browser)

hemisphere one half of the Earth. The northern hemisphere is the half that is north of the equator.

herbivore plant-eating animal

hominid member of the family of two-legged apes made up of humans and our fossil ancestors

hunter-gatherer person who obtains food by hunting, fishing and foraging rather than farming

ivory hard white material that forms the tusks of elephants

mammal warm-blooded animal that feeds its young on milk

marsupial type of mammal in which the young develop inside a pouch on the mother's body

microclimate pattern of weather within a small area, such as a valley, treetop or burrow

migration journey made by an animal to find a new home. Many animals migrate each year.

monsoon very rainy season in South Asia; or the wind that causes the rainy season

nomad person who travels from place to place in search of food and water, instead of settling permanently

nutrient any chemical that nourishes plants or animals, helping them grow. Plants absorb nutrients from the soil, while animals get nutrients from food.

palaeontologist scientist who studies fossils

perennial plant that lives for several years (*see also* annual)

pollen dust-like particles produced by the male parts of a flower

predator animal that catches and eats other animals

primate type of mammal that usually has grasping hands and forward-facing eyes. Most primates live in the trees of tropical forests.

protein one of the major food groups. It is used for building and repairing plant and animal bodies.

rainforest lush forest that receives frequent heavy rainfall

reptile cold-blooded animal such as a snake, lizard, crocodile or turtle that usually has scaly skin and moves either on its belly or on short legs

ruminant animal with a complex, multi-chambered stomach. One chamber, the rumen, contains micro-organisms that help digest tough plants.

savanna tropical grassland with scattered trees

scrub or scrubland alternative general names for shrubland

shrubland biome that mainly contains shrubs, such as the chaparral of California

species particular type of organism. Cheetahs are a species but birds are not, because there are lots of different bird species.

temperate having a moderate climate. Earth's temperate zone lies between the tropics and the polar regions.

tropic of Cancer imaginary line around the Earth 2600 km (1600 miles) north of the equator. From here, the sun is directly overhead at noon on 21 June.

tropic of Capricorn imaginary line around Earth 1600 miles (2600 km) south of the equator. From here, the sun appears directly overhead at noon on 21 December.

tropical between the tropics of Cancer and Capricorn. Tropical places are warm all year.

tropical forest forest in the Earth's tropical zone, such as tropical rainforest or monsoon forest

tropical grassland tropical biome in which grass is the main form of plant life

tundra biome of the far north, made up of treeless plains covered with small plants

ungulate type of mammal, such as a horse, elephant or antelope, that has hooves and eats plants

Further research

Books
Bourlière, François. *Tropical Savannas*. New York: Elsevier Science, 1992.
Bright, Michael. *South America Revealed*. New York: DK Publishing, 2001.
Capstick, Peter. *Death in the Long Grass*. New York: St. Martin's Press, 1992.
MacDonald, David. *The New Encyclopedia of Mammals*. London: Oxford University Press, 2001.
Reader, John. *Africa: A Biography of the Continent*. London: Penguin, 1998.
Schaller, George B. *Serengeti Lion*. Chicago: University of Chicago Press, 1976.
Sinclair, A.R.E. (editor). *Serengeti* and *Serengeti II*. Chicago: University of Chicago Press, 1995.

Websites
The Man-eaters of Tsavo: http://www.rtpnet.org/robroy/tsavo/tsavo.html
(The full text of a classic book about Africa's two most famous man-eating lions.)
Marsupials of Australia: http://www.australianwildlife.com.au/features/marsupials.htm
(A good place to find out more about Australia's weird and wonderful native mammals.)
Wild World: www.nationalgeographic.com/wildworld/terrestrial.html
(A National Geographic clickable world map, providing masses of information about the world's ecosystems.)

Index

Page numbers in *italics* refer to picture captions.

Picture credits